A TRAVELLER'S GUIDE TO

D-DAY
and the
BATTLE *for*
NORMANDY

THE INTERLINK BATTLEFIELD GUIDES

THE TRAVELLER'S GUIDES TO THE BATTLES AND BATTLEFIELDS OF WORLD WAR II is a new series of guidebooks that uses eyewitness quotes, then-and-now photographs, interviews with those who were there, and absolutely up-to-date information to recreate for the casual tourist and the military scholar alike the great battles and campaigns of World War II.

Carl Shilleto works as a specialist battlefield guide for one of the largest coach tour firms in the UK covering areas such as Normandy, Arnhem, Nijmegen, Oosterbeek, Anzio, Salerno, and Monte Cassino. As a writer, he is a specialist on the Normandy Campaign. His other works include *The Fighting Fifty-Second* and *Pegasus Bridge and the Merville Battery*. He also writes frequently for newspapers.

Michael Tolhurst is a specialist on the history of the US Army in Europe. His interest in the subject dates back fifty-five years to when Mr. Tolhurst's Royal Navy father piloted the craft that landed the US Rangers on Omaha Beach for their attack on the guns of Pointe du Hoc. At their first reunion after the war, the grateful Rangers officially adopted Michael Tolhurst as their mascot – a close association he has enjoyed ever since. Mr. Tolhurst is presently the Archivist for the Rothschild Bank in London. He has written numerous magazine articles and is also the author of *The Battle of the Bulge – First Blood*.

Also available in this series:

THE BATTLE FOR THE GERMAN FRONTIER
(September 1944 to January 1945) by Charles Whiting

To request our complete 44-page full-color catalog, please call us toll free at **1-800-238-LINK,** visit our website at **www.interlinkbooks.com**, or write to
Interlink Publishing
46 Crosby Street, Northampton, MA 01060
e-mail: info@interlinkbooks.com

A TRAVELLER'S GUIDE TO

D-DAY
and the
BATTLE *for*
NORMANDY

BY CARL SHILLETO AND MIKE TOLHURST

Interlink Books

An imprint of Interlink Publishing Group, Inc.

New York • Northampton

First published in 2000 by

INTERLINK BOOKS
An imprint of Interlink Publishing Group, Inc.
99 Seventh Avenue • Brooklyn, New York 11215 and
46 Crosby Street • Northampton, Massachusetts 01060
www.interlinkbooks.com

Library of Congress Cataloging-in-Publication Data

Shilleto, Carl.
   A traveller's guide to D-Day and the Battle for Normandy/
Carl Shilleto and Michael Tolhurst.
   p. cm. -- (The traveller's guides to the battles & battlefields of WWII)
Includes bibliographical references.
ISBN 1-56656-341-0 (pbk.)
   1. World War, 1939-1945--Battlefields--France--Normandy--
Guidebooks. 2. World War, 1939-1945--Campaigns--France--
Normandy. 3. Normandy (France)--Guidebooks. 4. Normandy
(France)--History, Military--20th century. I. Title: D-Day and the
Battle of Normandy. II. Tolhurst, Michael. III. Title. IV. Series.

D756.5.N6 S49 2000
940.54'21421--dc21   00-038330

Conceived and produced by Wordwright Publishing,
St Johns Road, Saxmundham, Suffolk IP17 1BE, England
Email:wordwright@clara.co.uk

Cover design: Ruth Shane, Text design: Ruth Shane
Maps: David Ashby, Series Editor: Charles Perkins

Printed and bound in Canada

CONTENTS

Metric Measures and Equivalents

Length
1 meter (m)= 1.0936 yd = 3.28 ft
1 kilometer (km)= 1000 m = 0.6214 mi

Temperature
Celcius°= 5/9 (F°-32°)
Fahrenheit°= 9/5C°+32°

INTRODUCTION

MAJOR GENERAL DWIGHT D. EISENHOWER, known as "Ike" to his friends and colleagues, received his third star on July 7, 1942. With this extra pip came the command of the entire Allied force for the seaborne invasion of North Africa, codenamed Operation Torch. The successful Combined Operation took place in November of that year and, coinciding with a successful counter offensive by the Russians in their homeland, finally proved that the forces of Hitler's mighty military machine were not invincible.

A conference was arranged for the Allied leaders: Roosevelt, Churchill, and Stalin and the Combined Chiefs of Staff met at Casablanca in January 1943. Stalin was unable to attend but he let it be known that he expected his allies to open a second front in northwest Europe during 1943. The Chiefs of Staff ruled out an invasion of northern Europe that year, but did, however, appoint Lieutenant General Morgan as Chief of Staff to the Supreme Allied Commander (COSSAC) with the task of preparing the detailed plans needed for an invasion of the continent. By way of compensation to the Russians it was agreed that, following the success of the campaign in North Africa, the Allies would invade Sicily and mainland Italy, thereby forcing the Germans to divert some of their resources away from the Russian front.

By February 1943, Ike had earned the respect of his coalition superiors and was promoted to full general. Later that year he commanded other successful operations in Sicily and Italy, which ultimately ensured his appointment as supreme commander of the Allied Expeditionary Force in the first week of December 1943.

The initial planning organization of COSSAC had served its purpose by January 1944 and the Supreme Headquarters of the Allied Expeditionary Force (SHAEF) was formed in its place. Under the supreme command of Eisenhower, Air Chief Marshal Tedder was appointed deputy supreme

From left to right: supreme allied commander, Dwight D. Eisenhower; commander-in-chief of the Allied ground forces, General Bernard L. Montgomery; and deputy supreme commander, Air Chief Marshal Sir Arthur Tedder in Normandy, June 1944.

commander; Lieutenant General Bedell Smith was to act as Chief of Staff; General Montgomery as commander in chief of the Allied ground forces; Admiral Sir Bertram Ramsay as naval commander-in-chief; and Air Chief Marshal Leigh-Mallory as air commander-in-chief. Together, with some 20,000 staff this headquarters mobilized, assembled, and also co-ordinated Operation Overlord – the greatest air, naval, and ground assault ever to be planned and executed.

During the first few months of 1944 the south of England was transformed into a giant military base. Over three million soldiers, sailors, and airmen were training to play their part in the invasion of Europe. Those that entered the top security transit camps were effectively cut off from the outside world. Headquarters staff officers carefully coordinated and recorded the movement of every unit to ensure that the planned movement and embarkation of the fighting troops and the transfer of their vital supplies would run with clockwork precision. With an initial assault force of over 170,000 men and 20,000 vehicles it was a logistical nightmare for the planners involved.

Operation Neptune was the codename given to the naval part of Overlord. Over 1,000 supply vessels and 4,124 landing ships and craft would be used to transport the combat troops and their equipment across the English Channel. For the protection of the naval convoys, and to help soften up the German coastal defenses by naval bombardment, an additional 1,213 warships would sail with the armada.

The Germans, of course, realized that the Allies would very soon try to open a second front in the west. Clever deceptions planned by the Allies had ensured that the Nazis did not know the precise location of the invasion so Hitler issued a numbered Weisungen [War Directive] that contained direct orders emphasizing the need to strengthen the Atlantic Wall and to protect the coastline of his Third Reich, which extended from Denmark down to the Spanish border.

EYEWITNESS

Coastal defenses under construction will be completed with all possible speed, and the establishment of additional coastal batteries and the laying of further obstacles on the flanks will be considered . . . . I expect all staffs concerned to exert every effort during the time which still remains in preparation for the expected decisive battle in the West.
Adolf Hitler, November 3rd, 1943

In November 1943 Hitler appointed "The Desert Fox," generalfeldmarschall Rommel, inspector general of the Atlantic Wall defenses. This brilliant commander, who had won so many victories during the first year of the desert war, was destined to face his old adversary, Montgomery, once again. Rommel was dismayed by the lack of defenses, particularly in the Calvados region of Normandy, and immediately ordered obstacles to be placed in four separate strips along all open beaches; layering the defenses in this fashion insured their effectiveness at all tide levels and conditions. Within five months, half a million obstacles and over four million mines covered the beaches as part of Hitler's Atlantic Wall. Barbed wire entanglements and mine fields were interspaced with scores of reinforced concrete pillboxes, bunkers, and fortifications. Strategically placed at various points along the coastline, coastal batteries were also constructed and camouflaged as a precaution against naval or air attack. To counter the increasing threat of an airborne assault, rows of stakes, nicknamed "Rommel's Asparagus," were placed in the open fields, and all low-lying areas of farmland and tidal areas along the coast and inland waterways were flooded. By the summer of 1944 Normandy was rapidly becoming the fortress that Rommel had envisaged. For Rommel believed, contrary to the views of his superior, Oberbefehlshaber Gerd von Rundstedt, that if the invasion force was to be stopped at all, it must be stopped on the beaches.

On the evening of June 4th, 1944, General Eisenhower left the confines of his "circus wagon," one of a small collection of trailers and tents that served as the SHAEF battle headquarters, to attend his nightly conference in the library of Southwick House. Outside, the rain lashed against the windows as Group Captain Stagg delivered his latest meteorological report to the Allied senior commanders. A nervous Stagg, only too aware of his responsibility, predicted a break in the weather front that would begin late in the evening of June 5th. This was better news, but the forecasted conditions were still below the level previously agreed as the minimum suitable for a major offensive. Eisenhower deliberated this news with his commanders: Tedder, Montgomery, Smith, Ramsay, and Leigh–Mallory. After each commander had said his piece Ike sat in silence for a few moments of quiet contemplation. Staring, trance-like, at the heavy oak table in front of him, he felt the burden of his command.

At last, acutely aware of the impact his decision would have on the lives of millions of people, General Eisenhower looked up toward his commanders and announced his decision: "I am quite positive we must give the order. I don't like it, but there it is . . .. I don't see how we can do anything else." Just over six hours later another conference was held to hear the latest meteorological report. Stagg reconfirmed his forecast of a break in the weather.

EYEWITNESS

I was, therefore, faced with the alternatives of taking the risks involved in an assault during what was likely to be only a partial and temporary break in the bad weather, or of putting off the operation for several weeks until tide and moon should again be favorable. Such postponement, however, would have been most harmful to the morale of our troops, apart from the likelihood of our losing the benefits of tactical surprise. At 0400 hours on June 5, I took the final and irrevocable decision: the invasion of France would take place on the following day.
General Dwight D. Eisenhower

The wheels of the Allied war machine had been set in motion. Nothing could now stop the surge of momentum that had been building up for months. The massive force moved inexorably toward the French coastline. The outcome of the invasion was now temporarily transferred from the generals and planners to those men who would feel the repercussion of any design or technical errors first. For the thousands of infantrymen and armored personnel, who had already spent up to thirty-six hours being tossed about in their landing craft, the misery caused by the turbulent waters of the Channel would continue for another day and night. Then, drenched and fatigued from the ordeal of their horrendous voyage, these young men would have to rely upon discipline, adrenalin, and sheer guts to keep them going as they exited their landing craft and ran forth into the bloody nightmare that awaited them on the beaches of Normandy.

They would not be alone in their hell, for on either flank of the landing beaches the airborne troops – the "Red Devils" of the British 6th Airborne Division, and the "All Americans" and "Screaming Eagles" of the American 82nd and 101st Airborne Divisions – would first descend from the night sky to wreak havoc among the German defenders.

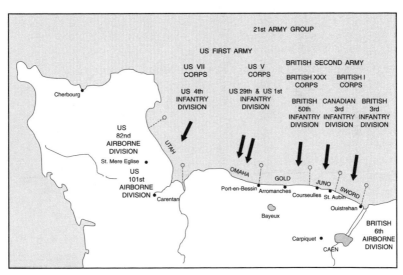

The D-Day landings, June 6th, 1944.

Getting There

THE BATTLE OF NORMANDY covers an area over 300 miles wide and 250 miles deep. The landing beaches alone stretch for over 45 miles. In order to understand the complex series of battles that made up the Normandy campaign, this book is divided into seven chapters. Each chapter starts with the D–Day landings on June 6th, 1944 and then expands to cover the areas captured by the advancing Allied armies.

At the end of each chapter, a suggested tour covers the main parts of the battlefield and highlights places of interest. Contact numbers for these places are listed at the end of this section, along with the numbers of local tourist information offices. We hope this will make your journey around the battlefields of Normandy as easy and as interesting as possible. But first, some advice on how to get there.

FOR U.S. AND CANADIAN VISITORS

Details of direct flights to France from the US and Canada can be easily obtained from your nearest international airport or from the French tourist information offices listed below. It would seem unlikely, however, that anyone travelling from the US or Canada would not want to visit the United Kingdom as part of their trip. The information listed in the next few pages, then, briefly details how to get to France via the UK.

For additional information on travelling, accommodation, and events in Normandy it is best to contact your nearest French Government Tourist Office, which can be found on the **www.franceguide.com** website.

One may also ask for detailed brochures at the following addresses.

For the US:

610 Fifth Avenue, Suite 222, New York, NY 10020–2452.

9454 Wiltshire Boulevard, Los Angeles, California
   90212–2967.

645 North Michigan Avenue, Chicago, Illinois 60611–2836.

1 Hallidie Plaza, Suite 250, San Francisco, California 94102–2818.

2305 Cedar Springs Road, Suite 205, Dallas, Texas 75201.

For Canada:

30 St Patrick Street, Suite 700, Toronto, Ontario M5T 3A3

For the UK:

178 Piccadilly, London W1V OAL.

TRAVEL TO FRANCE FROM THE UK

By Ferry: *Brittany Ferries.* The Brittany Centre, Wharf Road,
   Portsmouth PO2 8RU. Tel: 0990 360 360 (Portsmouth to Caen
   or St Malo; or Poole to Cherbourg).

Hoverspeed Fast Ferries. International Hoverport, Marine Parade,
   Dover CT17 9TG. Tel: 01304 240 088 (Dover to Calais; or
   Folkstone to Boulogne).

P&O European Ferries. Peninsula House, Wharf Road, Portsmouth
   PO2 8TA. Tel: 0990 980 555 (Portsmouth to Le Havre or
   Cherbourg).

P & O Stena Line. Channel House, Channel View Road, Dover
   CT17 9TJ. Tel: 0990 980 980 (Dover to Calais).

Sea France. Eastern Docks, Dover, Kent CT16 1JA. Tel: 01304
   240033 (Dover to Calais).

By Eurotunnel: Car carrying service Dover to Calais. Tel: 0990
   353 535

By Air: *Air France Group.* Colet Court, 100 Hammersmith Road,
   London W6 7JP. Tel: 0181 742 4488 (Gatwick to Caen).

Love Air. Building 44, First Avenue, Stanstead Airport CM24 1QE.
   Tel: 01279 681 434 (Birmingham to Caen).

By Coach: *Eurolines.* 52 Grosvenor Gardens, London SW1W
   OAU. Tel: 01582 404511. Regular coach services from London
   (with nationwide connections through National Express).

By Rail: *Eurostar.* Rail Europe Travel Centre, 179 Piccadilly,
   London, W1V 0BA. Tel: 0990 848 848.

The Battlefield Tourist might wish to start his tours from a base town. For the British sector, Caen or Bayeux are excellent starting places; for the American sector, we would suggest Bayeux, Carentan, or St. Mère Église. Alternatively, good accommodation can be found in many of the places mentioned in the tours themselves or from the information provided by the French Government Tourist Office.

MUSEUMS

Here is a list of the museums mentioned in the book. Their telephone numbers are included so that opening times can be checked. In addition, a few of the tourism offices located in Normandy are listed so that the Traveller may inquire about other places of interest in the area. Please note that all telephone numbers given are local numbers. To telephone these numbers from the UK, dial 00 33 and drop the first 0 on the local number. To telephone them from the US or Canada, dial 011 33 and drop the first 0 on the local number.

Arromanches. Musée du Debarquement (The D–Day Landings Museum). Tel: 02.31.22.34.31.

Arromanches. 360 Cinema. Tel: 02.31.22.30.30.

Bayeux. Musée Memorial de la Bataille de Normandie (The Battle of Normandy Memorial Museum). Tel: 02.31.92.93.41. Benouville, Pegasus Bridge, Café Gondrée Annexe. Tel: 08.02.40.13.28.

Caen. The Caen Memorial Un Musée pour la Paix (The Caen Memorial and Museum of Peace). Tel: 02.31.06.06.44.

Cherbourg. Musée de la Liberation (The Liberation Museum). Tel: 02.33.21.52.20.

Douvres-la-Deliverande. Musée Radar (The Radar Museum). Tel: 02.31.06.06.45.

Falaise. Musée Août 44 (The August 1944 Museum). Tel: 02.31.90.37.19.

Grandchamp–Maisy. Musée des Rangers (The Rangers Museum). Tel: 02.31.92.33.51.

Longues-sur-Mer. Batterie de Longues (The Longues Battery). Tel: 02.31.06.06.45.

Merville-Franceville. Musée de la Batterie de Merville (The Merville Battery Museum). Tel: 02.31.24.21.83.

Ouistreham. Musée No 4 Commando (The No 4 Commando Museum). Tel: 02.31.96.63.10.

Ouistreham. Musée du Mur de l'Atlantique (The Atlantic Wall Museum). Tel: 02.31.97.28.69.

Port-en-Bessin. Musée des Epaves sous–marines du Débarquement (The

Museum of Underwater Wrecks). Tel: 02.31.21.17.06.

Quinéville. Musée de la Liberté (The Museum of Freedom). Tel: 02.33.21.40.44.

St Laurent-sur-Mer. Musée Omaha – 6 juin 1944 (The Omaha Museum – June 6th, 1944). Tel: 02.31.21.97.44.

Sainte Marie-du-Mont. Musée du Débarquement – Utah Beach (The Utah Beach Landings Museum. Tel: 02.33.71.53.35.

St Martin-des-Besaces. Musée de la Percée du Bocage (The Bocage Breakthrough Museum). Tel: 02.31.67.52.78.

St Mère Église. Musée des Troupes Aéroportées (Airborne Troops Museum). Tel: 02.33.41.41.35.

Surrain. Musée de la Liberation (The Liberation Museum). Tel: 02.31.22.57.56.

Tilly-sur-Seulles. Musée de la Bataille de Tilly (The Battle of Tilly Museum). Tel: 02.31.80.80.26.

MAIN TOURISM OFFICES

Comité Départemental du Tourisme du Calvados,
Caen. Tel: 02.31.27.90.30.

Comité Départemental du Tourisme de la Manche,
St. Lô. Tel: 02.33.05.98.70.

Comité Départemental du Tourisme de l'Orne,
Alençon. Tel: 02.33.28.88.71.

Comité Régional de Tourisme de Normandie,
Evreux. Tel: 02.32.33.79.00.

LOCAL TOURISM OFFICES

Arromanches.	Tel: 02.31.22.36.45
Bayeux.	Tel: 02.31.51.28.28.
Caen.	Tel: 02.31.27.14.14.
Carentan.	Tel: 02.33.42.74.01.
Cherbourg.	Tel: 02.33.93.52.02.
Falaise.	Tel: 02.31.90.17.26.
Merville–Franceville.	Tel: 02.31.24.23.57.
Port–en–Bessin.	Tel: 02.31.21.92.33.
St Lô.	Tel: 02.33.05.02.09.
St Mère Église.	Tel: 02.33.21.53.91.

1
THE FLIGHT OF PEGASUS

THROUGHOUT THE NIGHT OF JUNE 5TH, 1944, over a thousand Allied bombers pounded the German defenses between Cherbourg and the mouth of the River Dives. Lancaster, Halifax, and Mosquito bombers transformed the lush Norman countryside into a lunar landscape. Shortly after midnight, amid the confusion and spectacle, three Horsa gliders crash-landed in a narrow triangular field that lay next to a swing bridge over the Caen Canal at Bénouville. Three assault platoons, commanded by Major John Howard of the 2nd Battalion, Oxfordshire & Buckinghamshire Light Infantry, stormed the bridge to overpower the German garrison in a coup de main operation.

As gunfire echoed around the bridge, the German defenders were caught by surprise. A Very light, fired by a German sentry, revealed camouflaged troops with blackened faces charging toward the bridge. Lieutenant Brotheridge stormed across the bridge with his platoon in full battle cry. The brilliant glare of the flare also revealed the sentry's position. Brotheridge cut him down with a sharp burst of fire from his Sten gun. The Germans returned fire. Within seconds Brotheridge, too, was mortally wounded – the first British soldier to spill his blood on French soil in the Normandy invasion.

A Horsa glider of the type that landed Major Howard and his men near Bénouville.

18

As the battle raged, another British attack was launched on the bridge over the River Orne. Within ten minutes both bridges had been captured and the troops began digging in and setting up a defense perimeter. Their orders were to await reinforcement from the rest of the 6th Airborne Division, which would soon be landing in and around the drop zones east of the River Orne. Also arriving soon would be the inevitable counter-attack by the Germans.

It was imperative that these two bridges remained intact and in British hands. If this could be achieved then the advancing Allied armies, already aboard their ships and nearing the Normandy coast, would better be able to establish and expand their own bridgehead after landing on the beaches at daybreak. The 6th Airborne area of operations would act as a pivot from which the Allied forces could sweep their way around from the Cotentin Peninsula, across the French countryside, toward the Seine and Paris and, ultimately, Hitler's Third Reich.

The Germans had been caught completely by surprise, not least the Bénouville garrison commander, Major Schmidt, who had decided to spend the evening in the nearby village of Ranville with his girlfriend. As commander of the garrison whose task it was to defend the bridges, Schmidt had not even put the demolition charges in place beneath the bridges that evening. Such nonchalance was evident straight up the German chain of command. Even Rommel, who had returned to Germany to try to persuade Hitler to release two more panzer divisions along his front, decided to combine his trip with a visit to his wife who was to celebrate her birthday on June 6th. Such were the conditions caused by the unsettled: no one, least of all the troops on the ground, expected an attack.

Major General "Windy" Gale, divisional commander of the British 6th Airborne, had several other tasks to complete before dawn, not least of which was silencing the heavily fortified German coastal battery at Merville. Despite a raid by a hundred Lancasters dropping 4,000-pound bombs, the guns of the battery were still undamaged beneath their massive reinforced concrete casemates. The task of destroying the guns was assigned to Lieutenant Colonel Terrance Otway, who would lead the men of the 9th Parachute Battalion (PB) on one of the most daring raids of the whole invasion. Despite the loss of their supplies and heavy equipment, and with over three-quarters of his paratroopers still missing after a disastrously scattered drop, Otway decided to attack the battery with his meager force.

EYEWITNESS

In the Parachute Regiment, giving up is not an option.
Lieutenant Colonel Otway, commander, 9th PB

Otway's command made its way through the darkened countryside to the battery's perimeter wire. Here they waited tensely for the arrival of three gliders, due to land within the grounds of the coastal battery. The surprise arrival of the gliders, loaded with combat troops, was expected to create panic and confusion among the 130-strong German garrison; Otway would then launch his assault across the barbed wire entanglements and minefields of the fortified perimeter defenses.

As the time of the attack approached, only two gliders could be seen circling above the battery (one having lost its tow shortly after take-off), but the star shells – which the ground troops would use to illuminate the

A Horsa glider of the 6th Airborne Division. With Horsas, it was sometimes difficult to distinguish between a landing and a crash.

area for the glider pilots – had been lost in the drop. Under fire from German anti–aircraft guns, one of the glider pilots mistook a nearby village for the battery and headed off in the wrong direction. The second glider headed for the battery but was caught in crossfire from German anti-aircraft guns, which caused the glider to overshoot its landing zone into a nearby orchard.

Otway decided to waste no more time and launched his attack. Two gaps were blown in the barbed wire with Bangalore torpedoes and his men charged through. In the confusion, many of the men ran over the uncleared minefield with the inevitable horrific results. Hand-to-hand fighting ensued and chaos and confusion seemed to reign. At this point, however, the months of hard training gave the attackers the edge and the German garrison was finally forced to surrender. After spiking the guns (which happened to be 100mm field guns and not the 150mm guns that had been predicted by Intelligence), Otway gave the order to withdraw. Only about 80 of the 150 men who had begun the assault were capable of walking out of the area with him. The rest lay dead or wounded.

Elsewhere, on the eastern flank of the 6th Airborne Division, the extent of the scattered parachute drops was becoming apparent. Many paratroopers had landed far from their designated drop zone and some of the least fortunate had landed in the flooded waters of the Dives Valley. Overburdened by their heavy equipment, which weighed in excess of thirty-five kilograms (eighty pounds), some subsequently drowned in the cold dark waters of the river.

EYEWITNESS

I found I was oscillating badly when my chute opened, rigging lines twisted as well. Remembering the drill, I kicked like mad and pulled down hard on my front lift webs. I thought I was reasonably in control, when splash, I'd landed in water! It was pitch black, I was flat on my back, being dragged by my canopy in water a foot or so deep. Struggling to release my parachute harness, and trying to keep my head above water, I lost my Sten gun. After freeing myself of the parachute I searched in vain for my gun. Getting accustomed to the light I waded to dry land. Lots of trees, so I realized that I was nowhere near the dropping zone allocated to 3rd Parachute Brigade H.Q. Company. I had no radio, no gun, no small pack, soaked to the skin, no idea which way I should go, but I did have eight Sten gun magazines in my pouches!
Signaller David "Dai" King, 53rd Airlanding Light Regiment, Royal Artillery

Spread over an area in excess of 500 square miles, several groups made up from men of various regiments and battalions, formed together to complete the other primary tasks essential to the success of the landings. As the 3rd Parachute Brigade headquarters were being set up on the high ground near Le Mesnil, the 5th Parachute Brigade began to establish its own headquarters in Ranville. From Ranville, the southern part of a ridge that ran in a semi-circle from the village of Sallenelles through Bréville and Le Mesnil toward Colombelles, would be taken and defended. Here reinforcements would assemble, ready to assist the gliderborne troops at the bridges over the River Orne and the Caen Canal. The bridge over the Orne was later renamed Pegasus Bridge in honor of the 6th Airborne; the bridge over the Caen Canal was renamed Horsa Bridge after the type of glider used in the landings.

The 7th PB, (which included a young officer, Richard Todd, an actor who had put his career on hold to join the Red Berets), had been reduced to less than a quarter of its strength as a result of the scattered drop. Without pause, the unit's commanding officer, Lieutenant Colonel Pine–Coffin, gave the order to move off to their objective, Bénouville, where they were to relieve Major Howard's men on the bridges.

Colombelles was taken and held but at the cost of numerous casualties. Despite this, the airborne troops continued to fight tenaciously and held their ground even after the seaborne forces and additional airborne reinforcements arrived later in the day.

Movie idol Richard Todd, a former Lieutenant in the 7th Parachute Battalion.

EYEWITNESS

"A" company at Bénouville, with all its officers killed or wounded, was to hold out for seventeen hours, even though reduced to a strength of less than twenty. From time to time we could hear an officer's voice rallying his troops with shouts of encouragement. We did not realize until later that he was lying wounded by the window of a house in the village, with one leg blown away.
Lieutenant Richard Todd, 7th PB

The 6th Airborne was also under orders to delay any German advance or counter-attack from the east. To achieve this, five bridges had been selected for demolition in the Dives valley. The bridges at Troarn, Varaville, and Robehomme, and two more at Bures, were all successfully destroyed by the Royal Engineers, who were supported by stragglers from various parachute battalions and units.

As late as 0500 on D-Day, after the capture of the Merville Battery and the blowing of the bridges over the River Dives and River Divette, von Rundstedt's headquarters was still in total confusion, unable to make sense of his field commanders' conflicting reports. Already the Luftwaffe had been sent to intercept the ghost invasion force in the Pas de Calais

Generalfeldmarschall Gerd von Rundstedt (right) with Obergruppenführer Sepp Dietrich.

(payloads of aluminium foil dropped over the channel had created that blip on the German's radar screens), while dummy parachutists gave the impression that the invasion was taking place between Le Havre and Rouen. The 21,000 strong 12th SS Panzer Division (Hitler Jugend)★, the 21st Panzer Division, and the Panzer Lehr Divisions were now on full alert but still awaiting orders as to where to strike.

As dawn broke, the breathtaking sight of thousands of Allied ships on the horizon combined with devastating naval and aerial bombardment insured that the German commanders nearest the landing beaches could have no doubt as to where the invasion would take place.

Several hours later British commandos, led by the eccentric aristocrat, Lord Lovat, made their way from Sword Beach to link up with the airborne troops at Pegasus Bridge. Wearing his green beret and distinctive white woollen pullover, Lovat strode, walking-stick in hand, toward the canal bridge. His men marched proudly toward the bridge as though oblivious to the mortar, shell, and sniper fire around them.

★ *It should be pointed out that Sturmbahnführer Bremer's Reconnaissance Battalion of the Hitler Jugend had already taken 6th Airborne paratroopers prisoner by 0130 and the divisional commander Brigadeführer [Brigadier General] Fritz Witt had guessed that this was the real thing.*

EYEWITNESS

I first knew that the invasion had begun with a report that parachutists had dropped near Troarn a little after midnight on 6 June. Since I had been told that I was not to make a move until I had heard from Rommel's headquarters, I could do nothing immediately but warn my men to be ready.
General Edger Feuchtinger, commander, 21st Panzer Division

Lovat's piper, Bill Millin, then began to play his bagpipes to signal the airborne troops of their arrival. After crossing both the bridges, the commandos moved on to strengthen the airborne troops on the high ground near Amfreville. The commandos and airborne troops took heavy casualties capturing and holding the ridge. By evening, after the arrival of the 6th Airlanding Brigade brought in by an awesome armada of over 250 gliders, the troops of the 6th Airborne Division had established a sizable bridgehead and additional supplies and reinforcements were already being

brought in over the Pegasus and Horsa Bridges.

In the days that followed, the 6th Airborne continued to fight off German counter-attacks and hold its front line. However, one area proved to be a constant thorn in the side of the divisional commander – the village of Bréville. Situated on high ground between the Château St. Côme and Amfreville, the Germans had consolidated their positions in Bréville and their resistance was proving too strong to penetrate. They enjoyed a commanding view of all the Allies' movements east of the River Orne and on the plain toward Caen. So long as the Germans held this high ground they threatened the Allied advance both east and south.

"Windy" Gale decided that this threat to his front line could no longer be tolerated. On June 10th, three battalions of the 51st Highland Division, (known as the "Highway Decorators" for the unceremonious daubing of their divisional "HD" sign on buildings where they had fought) were brought forward to reinforce Gale's depleted airborne troops. An attack against Bréville was put in at first light on June 11th by the 5th Battalion, The Black Watch. Having previously fought in the vast open spaces of the North African desert, the dense Norman Bocage disoriented the Scots. Attacking from the direction of the Château St Côme, through the lines held by Otway's 9th PB, they were massacred by a constant barrage of German mortars, machine guns, and SP (self-propelled) guns. With over 200 casualties, the Scots retreated totally demoralized. Later, Montgomery sacked their commander, Major General Erskine, for failing to inspire his men.

"Windy" Gale decided to change tactics. Using his reserve

Horsa gliders after landing on D-Day. Note special D-Day invasion stripes.

Bréville with a 13th/18th Hussars Sherman tank in the foreground. June 13th, 1944.

battalion (the 12th PB), a company from the 12th Devonshire Regiment, and a troop of Sherman tanks from the 13th/18th Hussars, he decided to catch the Germans off guard. This time he would launch an evening assault after a preliminary artillery bombardment. The troops made their way through the commando positions at Amfreville toward the start line in the nearby orchards. As the men waited nervously for the attack to begin, some of the shells and mortars fell short of the targets and landed among the waiting troops killing, among others, the commanding officer of 12th Para, Lieutenant Colonel "Johnny" Johnson. After a few terrifying minutes the barrage abruptly ceased. The attack on Bréville began.

The British troops, flanked by Sherman tanks, cautiously advanced across the waist-high cornfields toward the shattered and burning remains

EYEWITNESS

We were on our feet and continued our advance . . . . On our way we passed many dead and a stream of our men coming back toward us: bloody faces, limp arms, staggering and weaving. Some collapsed and remained still, some crawled on hands and knees.
Major Simm, second in command, 12th PB

of the village. Swirls of thick acrid smoke polluted the air and hung in a pall above the devastated German defenses. The German soldiers initially fought back but soon realized their position was untenable and began retreating. Bréville was soon in the hands of the airborne troops.

In the center of the village, the crossroads and village green were covered with a tangled mass of German weapons and partially buried corpses. Illuminated by the flickering light of the burning church and

The morning after the battle, 6th Airborne troops in Bréville.

houses, the scene was further dramatized by an eerie lament from the church organ as the flames fanned air through its pipes.

As the troops began to set up their defenses, a password was relayed, back to headquarters to lay down defensive fire while the troops consolidated their positions. The password was misinterpreted over the crackling wireless set, however, and seconds later a second pre–assault barrage was fired into the shattered remains of Bréville. For the second time that evening British troops were killed and wounded by friendly fire, though some of the more fortunate managed to find protection in nearby craters and ditches. When silence returned and the dust settled Colonel Parker, deputy commander of the 6th Airlanding Brigade, set up a command post in the village. There, among the carnage from a week of fighting, the airborne troops and the tanks of the 13th/18th Hussars dug in against the expected German counter-attack. It never came. On this part of the front at least, German resolve had been broken. The Bréville gap had finally been closed and the 6th Airborne Division's bridgehead was now secure.

As the American, British, and Canadian Armies advanced southward into the Norman countryside through the rest of June, July, and into August, the 6th Airborne Division remained static; holding the line but constantly penetrating the German lines with reconnaissance patrols. The Germans continued to counter-attack along the front but each time were repulsed. Nevertheless, constant shelling and mortaring by the Germans took a steady toll of about 300 casualties per week. Not until Caen had fallen and the Canadian offensive, Operation Tractable, had been launched and was finally pushing the German forces back toward Falaise did the 6th Airborne Division receive orders to drive the Germans back over the River Dives.

On August 7th, Gale had been informed by his commander, Lieutenant General Crocker of I Corps, that the Germans were preparing to withdraw and that Gale and his men must drive them back toward the mouth of the River Seine. This would not only protect the left flank of the Canadian offensive but, by keeping pressure on the retreating Germans, the Canadians could also accelerate their advance toward the Falaise and the Seine.

Reinforced with a Dutch and a Belgian brigade, and commandos from No. 1 and No. 4 Special Service Brigades, the airborne division began their offensive across the flooded meadows of the Dives valley. Aptly named Operation Paddle, the offensive began on August 17th after the Germans were finally seen retreating. With much of the area still underwater (a legacy of Rommel's anti-invasion defenses), Gale chose to make his main advance along a route that ran from Troarn toward Dozulé and Putot en Auge. From here the advance would continue over the River Touques at Pont L'Évêque; through Beuzeville, Pont Audemer, over the River Risle, and finally to the mouth of the River Seine.

At the same time the 6th Airlanding Brigade, the Dutch Princess Irene Brigade, and the Belgian Piron Brigade would move northeastward through their front line at Sallenelles toward Merville and begin clearing the remaining German positions along the coast toward Cabourg. To the east, No. 1 Special Service Brigade attacked Bavent as the Canadian paratroopers moved from Le Mesnil through the Bois de Bavent. In Bures the 3rd Parachute Brigade crossed the river (though this was delayed as the Royal Engineers had to rebuild the bridge they had destroyed back on June 6th). To the south No. 4 Special Service Brigade took Troarn and advanced toward Dozulé.

The 3rd Parachute Brigade made swift progress from Bures until they came to the deep tidal canal between Goustranville and Putot en Auge. As the area was under German observation from the heights around Putot en Auge, Gale decided to launch a night offensive and to coordinate his attack with the 5th Parachute Brigade, which had been held in reserve.

Late on the evening of August 18th, the 3rd Parachute Brigade launched their offensive on the four bridges over the Dives Canal (now called Le Grand Canal). After four hours of fighting, all four bridge sites had been captured, with the Germans only managing to completely destroy two of the bridges. The 3rd Parachute Brigade crossed the canal and advanced to the railway line that was the start line for the second offensive. The 5th Parachute Brigade then leap-frogged the 3rd and launched their attack on the village of Putot en Auge. Here they met strong opposition and a determined German rearguard on the heights in and around Putot en Auge, which overlooked the main road (now N-175) from the south.

The 9th Parachute Brigade (commanded by Major Napier Crookenden after Lieutenant Colonel Otway had been concussed and later evacuated) managed to cross the damaged railway bridge over the canal (now replaced by the A-13 Autoroute de Normandie bridge) and moved on to take the nearby railway station. By the time 13th Parachute Battalion of the 5th Parachute Brigade had arrived, the incoming tide had caused the water level to rise, making any crossing too hazardous to attempt. Instead, the 13th used the second bridge that had been captured by the 1st Canadian PB and moved toward their start line along the railway line. Here they were to remain in reserve until the 7th PB had taken its objective east of Putot en Auge. In the meantime, the 12th PB, on the right flank, would take the village. The 13th would then proceed through the 7th's positions and take the high ground beyond, known as Hill 13, which overlooked Dozulé.

The 7th PB, commanded by Lieutenant Colonel Pine-Coffin, encountered some German anti-tank positions as they made their way toward their objective. Dealing with these defenses and the ambush of a German patrol delayed their advance for more than an hour. More time was lost circumventing some of the impenetrable hedgerows. By the time the 7th crossed the railway line, daylight was beginning to creep across the horizon. The troops hastened their advance, but as they made their way along a hedgerow they were spotted by a German observer. Lieutenant Thomas of "B" Company was leading his platoon at the head of the battalion's advance when a machine gun opened fire. He fell, seriously wounded, and the rest of the men dove for cover. The company was now pinned down behind the hedgerow. A section was immediately dispatched to neutralize the machine gun. When this was accomplished, the company prepared to move on it was reported that troops had been seen advancing across a field to their left heading directly for their position.

Since he was now running behind schedule, Pine-Coffin assumed that it was the men of the 13th PB approaching in preparation for their advance through his position. But as the advancing figures approached through the twilight and morning mist it became apparent that they were German. This time the hedgerow worked to the advantage of the British, concealing the paras from the advancing patrol. They hastily prepared an ambush and waited for the Germans to walk into their trap. Pine-Coffin could have ordered the massacre of the patrol but instead decided to give the unsuspecting Germans a chance to surrender. Lieutenant Mills, who spoke fluent German, ordered the enemy troops to halt and lay down their weapons. The unsuspecting Germans stopped in their tracks and looked around in astonishment. Totally flustered, they tried to assess their predicament. One of the German soldiers decided to deal with the situation himself and threw himself to the ground, firing his machine gun into the hedgerow. The paras returned fire with a devastating enfilade. The Germans who survived the onslaught surrendered or ran back into the gloom of the early dawn.

The 7th PB then continued their advance and managed to take their objective without encountering any further difficulties. In the meantime, the 12th PB attacked and captured Putot en Auge taking 120 Germans prisoner.

As the 13th PB moved up to begin their attack on Hill 13, they had to cross over half a mile of open country in daylight. With no other cover available, Lieutenant Colonel Peter Laurd explained to his company commanders that their only option was to run like hell across the open space and hope that the German observers, not expecting such a bold maneuver, would be slow in responding. The gamble paid off. Most of the battalion got across safely before the Germans opened fire and wounded half a dozen paras. "A" Company immediately launched an assault up the hill while "C" Company attacked on the flank. The paras charged into the German positions with bayonets fixed, but as soon as they reached the top of the hill German reinforcements launched a fierce counter-attack.

Most of the men in the leading assault platoons from "A" Company were killed or wounded and the remaining support platoons were forced back down the hill, then up and over onto the reverse slope of a nearby ridge. The paras took cover in the grassy slopes of the ridge and waited for the advancing Germans to come into view. An artillery officer, who had crossed the open ground in his Bren gun carrier, immediately called on his gunners to lay down a barrage. The shellfire stopped the Germans barely 100 yards from the paras' positions. Seizing the initiative, Lieutenant Colonel Laurd ordered "C" Company to launch an attack on the German right flank but the Germans were already prepared for such an attack with a well-situated machine gun and "C" Company was unable to make any headway. With the ridge offering a commanding view of the German positions Brigadier Nigel Poett, commander of the the 5th Parachute Brigade, ordered the 13th PB to consolidate their defenses and dig in.

The battle for Putot en Auge had been successful and the paras had accounted for over 200 German troops and a substantial amount of enemy equipment. The paras themselves had sustained 114 casualties and the troops were now exhausted, having been in action for nearly forty-eight hours.

EYEWITNESS

So we stayed where we were. I had a company commanders' meeting and in the middle of it, so tired was I, that I went to sleep as I was actually talking. They left me sleeping and left word that I was not to be disturbed. I woke up two hours later and the meeting was resumed with my apologies.
Lieutenant Colonel Peter Laurd, commander, 13th PB

The paras held their positions, under constant shell and mortar fire, for the rest of the day, which added to their growing list of casualties. As evening approached on August 19th, the commandos prepared to take over the advance. Mills-Robert's No. 1 Special Service Brigade moved north to the area around Brucourt in order to mop up any remaining German resistance. No. 4 Special Service Brigade launched an attack on Hill 13, with No. 46 RM (Royal Marine) Commando leading the assault. Since there was no moonlight that evening, their journey across the fields and through the thick hedgerows and small copses, was slow and ponderous with the officers having to rely on their compass bearings to navigate. As the commandos began their ascent of the hill they came across a badly wounded German soldier who had been left behind after the fighting the previous morning. As the wounded soldier was lying just in front of the German positions, there was a danger the Allied position would be compromised, so one of the officers crept forward and silenced him.

The commandos then moved on. As they came to the top of the hill, the night sky was illuminated by a Very light and a German machine gun opened fire. Blue and green tracer fire flashed above the heads of the commandos as they lay prostrate, but the Germans had clearly not seen them and the firing eventually subsided. Captain Pierce then ordered his men in the lead troop to storm the hilltop. After the hill was captured, and reinforced by the rest of the brigade, No. 48 (RM) Commando pushed on to occupy and set up their headquarters on another piece of high ground just past Dozulé. It was decided that with the Commando units under strength Dozulé was too heavily defended to attack.

General Gale, meanwhile, moved the 6th Airlanding Brigade from their positions near Cabourg and pushed on, bypassing Dozulé. Then, in the early hours of August 21st, the sky above Dozulé began to glow as orange and yellow flames rose from the village. The Germans had decided to retreat and razed the village to the ground as they left. The commandos moved in and occupied what was left.

Passing through the commandos, the 6th Airborne Division Armored Reconnaissance Regiment pressed on with the aid of their Cromwell tank squadron. Also in support were the Dutch and Belgian Reconnaissance units. The reconnaissance units continued to drive the Germans back until they encountered a stiff German rearguard at the village of Annebault. The terrain in this part of Normandy was ideal for defense with heavily wooded areas, rolling hills, and steep valleys. Despite being supported by armor and artillery, the German positions were eventually overrun when the 3rd Parachute Brigade launched an attack on the village.

The recce units then moved up through Annebault and advanced toward Pont L'Évêque. In morning sunshine along the route the troops were greeted by the local French, who were overjoyed at the departure of the Germans and eager to show their gratitude by plying their liberators with fresh milk, cakes, fruit, and Calvados – the potent local brew.

They reached Pont L'Évêque by midday on August 22nd, and the 5th Parachute Brigade prepared for an attack. The terrain around and in the village made it obvious that this was not going to be an easy battle. On the main road from Caen, the village is nestled in a valley with hills on either side that rise to over 130 meters (400 feet). The River Touques divides itself and flows through the village in two separate channels 70 meters apart. On the eastern side of the village, a railway line ran along an embankment from which the whole valley could be observed and, in the village itself, the narrow streets were lined with ancient timbered buildings that could very easily be set alight.

EYEWITNESS

We spoke to them and they clustered round. They told us of the horrors of Boche occupation . . . the Boche's manner: their possessiveness and the underlying fear of the sadistic cruelty in them that the French hated . . . [a] girl's father had quite suddenly been seized and put into a concentration camp, and her eldest brother had soon followed him. The blessed relief of freedom which our advance had brought touched them deeply. These Norman folk were not over-demonstrative, but their hearts were sound and brave.
Major General Richard "Windy" Gale, CB, DSO, OBE, MC, GOC 6th Airborne Division.

The plan was for the 13th PB to establish a bridgehead across both channels of the river, while the 12th would attempt to cross the shallow fords believed to be south of the village and take the railway embankment and the area known as St Julianê. The assault was to take place in the evening, but Gale, acting on recently gathered intelligence, believed that German movement was scarce enough to warrant an immediate attack in daylight. A smoke screen and artillery barrage were laid down and the assault began in the mid-afternoon.

With "A" Company in the lead, the 12th PB moved off across the open ground in search of the fords. As they approached the river they came under German fire. Despite a search they could not locate the fords. Unable to inform battalion headquarters of their predicament (because their wireless set had been hit), Captain Baker led nine of his men to the water's edge and swam across the river while the remainder of his company sheltered in the ditches. "B" Company, which was following up, was pinned down by machine gun fire from the overlooking hills on the eastern side of the valley and was unable to make any progress.

Captain Baker and his small assault force were having more success and had managed to dislodge the Germans from the railway embankment, but they soon ran short of ammunition. With the smoke screen now dispersing, Captain Baker gave the order to pull back, and as the men swam back across the river the Germans re-occupied the railway embankment. With two companies pinned down on their start line, Brigadier Poett called off the attack and the paras had to sit tight until nightfall before they could withdraw. The attack had cost the 12th PB fifty-six casualties.

In the meantime, the 13th PB had crossed the first river bridge in the village. The Germans, however, were well-positioned along the main street and had used incendiary bombs to set fire to some of the buildings hampering the para's advance. As the paras struggled to fight their way through the village, Royal Engineers hastily constructed a ford over the western branch of the river by pushing rubble into the water using an armored bulldozer. Once the ford was completed, four Cromwell tanks from the reconnaissance regiment crossed the river and took up positions around the church, engaging German machine gun posts and pillboxes on the far bank of the river. During this fighting one of the tanks was knocked out by a German anti–tank gun.

The raging fire and intense heat from the surrounding buildings was beginning to make life particularly uncomfortable for both paras and tank crews alike. Unable to make any headway across the eastern bridge, the Allies decided to set up a defensive perimeter where the fire was less fierce and wait for the flames to subside before launching any further attack.

The 13th PB had lost thirty-nine men that day. Though no record of the total number of casualties for the Germans was kept, it was later discovered that at least 127 had been killed during the fighting and that the German medics had been working throughout the night collecting the wounded from the ruins of the village.

By the following morning the fire had died down and another attack was in preparation. A reconnaissance patrol was able to cross the eastern part of the river and it was decided that there was a good chance that a bridgehead could be established. Immediately, the 13th PB was ordered to cross the river. All that remained of the bridge was a twenty-four meter (eighty foot) length of steel girder that was only twenty centimeters (eight inches) wide. Despite this, the men managed to cross and the street fighting began. By midday the German resistance was again proving too strong and well-established to infiltrate and the Germans were also constantly counter-attacking. With the town once again in flames, this time behind the advancing paratroopers, there was a chance that the paras could become cut off. Poett decided to send the 7th PB forward to establish a firm base so that the 13th could pull back and reorganize.

Throughout the night the 7th PB actively patrolled across the river and discovered that the Germans had finally decided to withdraw and were now in retreat, leaving behind them a trail of demolished bridges and cratered roadways.

Using the Pont Audemer road (N-175) as their main axis, the 6th Airborne Division moved forward, meeting more opposition when they reached Beuzeville. To the north the coastal areas had been cleared by the 6th Airlanding Brigade, with the help of the Dutch and Belgian brigades, and the unit had reached the mouth of the River Touques at Trouville. The whole division was now advancing along a sixteen-kilometer (ten-mile) front, hoping that a final push on the night of August 25th toward Pont Audemer would cut off those German troops retreating from the Allied formations pushing up from the south. Though no large numbers of Germans were captured, Pont Audemer was taken and by August 27th a line had been secured that stretched from the town, along the River Risle, and up to the coast.

The Germans had been pushed back across the River Seine and the seventy-two kilometer (forty-five mile) advance of the division had liberated more than 650 square kilometers (400 square miles) of Normandy. Lieutenant General Crerar sent his congratulations to the commander of the 6th Airborne Division:

EYEWITNESS

Desire you inform Gale of my appreciation immense contribution 6 Airborne Division and all Allied contingents under his command have made during recent fighting advance: the determination and speed with which his troops have pressed on in spite of all enemy efforts to the contrary have been impressive and of greatest assistance to the army as a whole.
Signal sent from Lieutenant General Crerar, commander of the First Canadian Army, to Lieutenant General J Crocker, commander of I British Corps.

The 6th Airborne Division returned to England during the first week of September to prepare for their next operation. During nearly three months of fighting in Normandy, the division had suffered 4,450 casualties of whom 821 were killed, 2,709 wounded, and 927 listed as missing.

CIRCUIT ONE

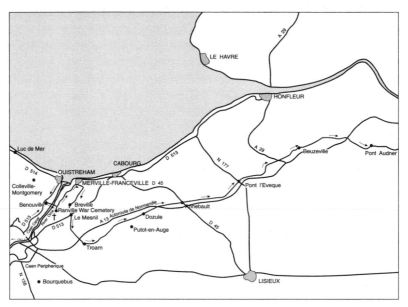

Circuit one. Caen-Bénouville-Merville.

F ROM THE PORT OF CAEN (Ouistreham) take the D-514 to Bénouville. Alternatively, if staying in Caen, take the D-515 to Ouistreham then follow the signposts for Bénouville, which will take you onto the D-514. Go straight across the roundabout/rotary in Bénouville and make use of the parking lot (kindly provided free of charge by Madame Arlette Gondrée) on the right hand side of the road, just before the Café Gondrée.

From here you may pay a visit to the Café Gondrée (between March and November), the first house to be liberated in the Normandy landings. Inside there is a wealth of memorabilia, photographs, and exhibits donated by veterans of the 6th Airborne Division, as well as a wide range of books and souvenirs for sale. In addition, the Café Gondrée Annexe will provide additional exhibits for viewing as well as a conference and briefing room for visitors, schools, and colleges when it opens.

Opposite the Café Gondrée, next to the café and Restaurant Les 3 Planeurs [The 3 Gliders] is a centaur A-27M Cromwell tank. Across the new Pegasus Bridge (the original is next to the site for the new Airborne Museum on the east bank of the canal) there are three memorials that mark the site of the original glider landings, as well as a bronze bust of Major John Howard who led the 2nd Battalion Oxford and Buckinghamshire Light Infantry and attached Royal Engineers in the capture of Pegasus Bridge. In addition, numerous memorials (including one at Horsa Bridge, over the River Orne, 400 yards further along the D-514) dedicated to the men and units that fought in this area dot the immediate vicinity.

From the parking lot take the D-514 across Pegasus Bridge and Horsa Bridge, then take the second exit on the roundabout signposted Ranville (D-37). Head toward the church in the center of the village (clearly visible from the road) and drive counter-clockwise around the church wall and park opposite the entrance to Ranville War Cemetery. A walk around this part of the village will again reveal memorials and information notice boards about the 6th Airborne Division and their operations.

Over 2,500 Commonwealth soldiers are buried in the cemetery, which also includes 322 Germans (far left corner). The majority of the 6th Airborne Division's dead now rest here and this war cemetery is still often referred to as the "Airborne Cemetery." In the churchyard, around the inside of the perimeter wall, there are more burials of Commonwealth soldiers, including the final resting place of Lieutenant Brotheridge, who was fatally wounded at Pegasus Bridge. The rebuilt church (the original was destroyed during the fighting around Ranville) also has a beautiful stained glass window dedicated to the airborne troops.

Madame Arlette Pritchett-Gondrée outside the Café Gondrée, the first house to be liberated in the Normandy landings.

From Ranville drive back to the roundabout/rotary on the D-514, take the next exit on your right (still the D-514) and continue along the road. At the top of the hill, to your right, is a vast open area of arable farming land. This was one of the four main drop and landing zones used by the 6th Airborne Division and the area where the 5th Parachute Brigade and 6th Airlanding Brigade landed on June 6th, 1944. It is here that each year, on the anniversary of the landings, the Parachute Regiment organizes a parachute drop and display on this drop zone which, until recently, used to include D–Day veterans.

Continue along the D–514 and into Sallenelles. This is where the Belgian Piron Brigade first went into action. A memorial on a stone pillar, about thirty-five meters (100 feet) on the left after the crossroads, is dedicated to the first Belgian soldier killed in Normandy. 450 meters (a quarter of a mile) beyond Sallenelles, as you continue toward Merville-Franceville-Plage, there is the former German radar station, which has now been transformed into a nightclub and discothéque called *Le Surfer*.

An interesting diversion for the Battlefield Tourist is a visit to the massive German concrete bunkers that are dotted all along the shoreline just before Merville. Take the first turn on the left signposted Base Nautique de Franceville. Continue along the narrow road and track until you arrive at the parking lot in the Estuaire de L'Orne. From here the concrete bunkers can clearly be seen still dominating the mouth of the estuary.

Return to the D–514 and continue into Merville. At the first set of traffic lights follow the signs for Musée de la Batterie de Merville. Park in in front of the museum, in the circular area around the memorial to the men of the 9th PB. The No. 1 casemate of this former German coastal gun emplacement has now been turned into an excellent museum (open April to October) that includes weapons, uniforms, and other memorabilia. There is also a selection of books, videos, and other souvenirs on sale.

Upon leaving the museum turn right, then right again, onto the D–223 until this road reaches the crossroads in Bréville. This was the scene of bitter and costly fighting by the 51st Highland Division, the 13th/18th Hussars, and the airborne troops. From the crossroads you can appreciate why the Germans were reluctant to give any ground here: this area offers a commanding view over Ranville, the bridges, and the land beyond. In the churchyard, next to the crossroads, there are the graves of two men from the 6th Airborne Division (the rest are buried in Ranville War Cemetery). When visiting any village in Normandy, look out for a white and green Commonwealth War Graves Commission plaque beside the entrance to a cemetery or churchyard. This signifies that Commonwealth troops are buried somewhere in the grounds.

At the crossroads turn left (D–37b) past the Château St Côme to the next crossroads at Le Mesnil. This was the area held by the 1st Canadian PB who, during the static period up until the breakout in August, held this area against heavy German counter-attacks. This area was also where the 3rd Parachute Brigade set up their headquarters in the pottery to the right and the 224th Parachute Field Ambulance set up their Main Dressing Station in a farm adjacent to the pottery. In just fourteen days beginning on June 6th, the medics here carried out over 112 major operations and treated over 800 casualties.

Continue to drive straight over the crossroads (still the D-37b) and turn left at the end of the road (D-37) and follow the signs for Troarn. Turn left at the crossroads in Troarn and drive through the village along the N-175 (on the right in the village is the local tourist information center signposted Syndicat d'Initiative). Continue to the bridge over the River Dives at St Samson. This is the site of one of the four bridges destroyed by the Royal Engineers on D-Day to delay the Germans from counter-attacking the airborne troops. This was also the route, (and from Bures two kilometers to the north), from which Lieutenant General Richard Gale launched his offensive during the breakout.

Continue along the N-175 toward Dozulé. The nearby village of Putot en Auge can be reached by taking a right turn onto the D-49. At the town hall in Putot en Auge there is a memorial plaque, unveiled on the 50th anniversary of the action there, dedicated to the 6th Airborne Division. Beyond the village, to the east, is Hill 13, which was eventually taken by the Commandos.

Return to the D-175 and continue east through Dozulé and Annebault. You are now using the same road along which the 6th Airborne Division Armored Reconnaissance Regiment led the way in their Cromwell tanks in the advance toward Pont L'Évêque. Though many of the black and white timber buildings in the village were destroyed during the fighting, some have been restored, including the church around which the tanks of the recce squadron and paras fought as they tried to push the Germans back. Also in Pont L'Évêque is another tourist information office, from which details of accommodation and sites of interest can be obtained.

From Pont L'Évêque you can follow the route, along the N-175, that the 6th Airborne Division took through Beuzeville to their final battle at Pont Audemer. Today there is little evidence of the skirmishes and battles that took place. What is still visible is the terrain and farm land over which the Allied troops had to fight forcing the Germans to retreat. Though the bomb and shell craters have long since been filled in, the countryside, in places, still remains much as it was back in 1944.

2

THE "ALL AMERICANS" AND THE "SCREAMING EAGLES" DESCEND

THE ORIGINAL D-DAY MISSION of the 82nd ("All American") and 101st ("Screaming Eagles") Airborne Divisions was very ambitious – more so, perhaps, than that of their British counterpart, the 6th Airborne Division, to the east. The Americans' mission was to cut the Cotentin Peninsula in half and at the same time secure forward positions so that the troops landing on Utah would be able to get off the beach and move inland. As early as June 1943 the Germans had flooded the low-lying fields behind Utah beach as an anti-invasion barrier. In some places the water was three to four feet deep.

The only access to the beaches across these flooded fields was by means of small causeways. By the end of May 1944, Allied intelligence had discovered that the Germans had reinforced their forces on the peninsula by adding the 91st Airlanding Division to the garrison in the area of Carentan.

This caused the US VII Corps to scale down their original plan. The mission of the 82nd Airborne was now to drop and secure both banks of the River Merderet and to hold the bridges south and west of the town of St Mère Église. With any forces available, they would then try to expand west and stop any German reinforcements from entering the area. The 101st would now drop further east and secure the Utah beach exits, of which there were four; at the same time, they would protect the southern flank of the invasion by holding the roads and rail bridge over the Douve river north of Carentan.

As the last light of June 5th began to dim, thousands of paratroopers, their faces blackened, waddled out to their

General Eisenhower talks informally to troops of the 101st Airborne prior to take-off.

respective planes. The same thing was happening at over twenty different airfields scattered around England. The men were wearing their distinctive tan two-piece jump suits, high-legged Corcoran boots, and carried a vast array of weapons, rations, ammunition, gadgets, plus of course their parachutes. Most of the paratroopers were carrying more than of 100 pounds.

General Eisenhower, the supreme commander, felt an almost personal responsibility for the fate of these men, and went off that evening to one of their bases, Greenham Common, to wish them well. There he walked and talked among the young men of the 101st Airborne.

EYEWITNESS

We saw hundreds of paratroopers, with blackened and grotesque faces, packing up for the big hop and jump. Ike wandered through them, stepping over packs, guns, and a variety of equipment such as only paratroops can devise, chinning with this and that one. All were put at ease.
Captain Harry Butcher, aide to General Eisenhower

Feeling more at ease, with coffee drunk and cigarettes extinguished, the men climbed aboard their transport planes. These were C-47 Skytrains, the workhorse of the US Army Air Force. Powered by two 1200 horsepower Pratt and Whitney engines, they could each carry about twenty-seven fully-equipped assault troops.

Just after midnight on June 6th, eighteen teams of Pathfinders,

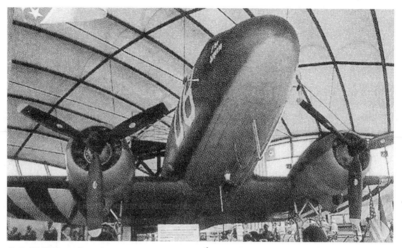

A C-47 "Skytrain" in the museum at St Mère Église.

volunteers from the 82nd and 101st, parachuted into Normandy. Their purpose was to mark the drop zones for the rest of the airborne assault. They were to set up special lights in the shape of the letter "T" and send out homing signals on their direction finder radios.

Brigadier General James M. "Jumpin Jim" Gavin told them, "When you land in Normandy you will have only one friend. God!"

The C-47 transport planes carrying the Pathfinders approached from the west. They came in too fast, and to add to the troubles there was a thick cloud bank over the area. This caused the pilots to fly too high or too low in order to avoid it. At the same time German anti-aircraft gunners opened up with their vast array of flak batteries. For many pilots it was their first time under fire and the young and inexperienced pilots started throwing their transport planes into violent evasive actions. As a result, only one team of Pathfinders landed in the correct spot. The rest were scattered over a wide area. One team missed land altogether and ended up in the sea.

Behind the Pathfinders came the main force of Major General Maxwell Taylor's 101st Airborne Division and Major General Matthew Ridgway's 82nd. They were packed into nearly 900 aircraft, flying in tight, nine-plane "V" formations. For over two hours the planes droned on, out over the channel, flying low to avoid German radar, and picking up route markers as they went along. The planes swung southeast, gained height to avoid flak from the Channel Islands, then dropped again as they crossed the western Cotentin coast. Strict radio silence had been observed, so no one got the message that the area was shrouded in cloud.

Immediately on beginning their drop run the C-47s were lost in the dense mist. Pilots never before confronted with flying in such tight formations lost sight of each other and panicked. Up and down, left and right they went, anywhere they could get clear vision and eliminate the risk of a mid-air collision. At the same time, anti-aircraft fire came up at them compounding their fears. One trooper remembers hearing, "Stand up and hook up; it's safer than sitting down."

Hardly any planes were at the correct height or speed in order to drop their men safely, but still, the green jump lights above the doors flicked on. It might not be the exact drop zone, but it was the Cotentin – and that was good enough for the pilots.

Chaos reigned in the skies. Planes were being hit, exploding, or crashing to the ground in flames. Anti-aircraft fire rose like a solid wall from the ground. In between all this, paratroopers were being hurled to the floor of their aircraft and cursing the pilots. Eager to get away from the aircraft, the men sometimes jumped blindly, only to find themselves floating down by parachute wondering what they had let themselves in for, and if it was all worth that few extra dollars a week of jump pay. Sergeant Louis Truax saw his plane's left wing hit, and then the paratroopers went sprawling.

EYEWITNESS

One man dived out the door headfirst. I grabbed the ammo belt of the man I thought next and gave him a heave out nose first. The next man made it crawling . . . then I dived.
Sergeant Louis Truax, US Airborne

A little over an hour later most of the men were on the ground, spread far and wide, hopelessly lost, and miles from their assigned drop zones. Some had been dropped far out to sea; others had been dropped so low that their parachutes hadn't opened. Private Donald Burgett recalled that the unlucky ones "made a sound like large, ripe pumpkins being thrown down against the ground." Those that survived the drop started to gather in the small dark fields and hedgerows, challenging each other. In the 101st, the men were issued a small tin plate child's toy, called a "cricket." One click was to be answered by two clicks. The 82nd

EYEWITNESS

"God must have opened the chute." [Reaction on being dropped from an altitude of 500 feet]. "When I began to use my cricket, the first man I met in the darkness I thought was a German until he 'cricketed.' He was the most beautiful soldier I'd ever seen, before or since. We threw our arms around each other, and from that moment I knew we had won the war."
Major General Maxwell Taylor, commander, 101st Airborne Division

had opted for a password, "Flash" which was to be answered by "Thunder."

So scattered were the troopers of the 82nd and the 101st that many fought alone or in small groups; often men from different divisions fighting alongside each other. There was one other mission both divisions had, and that was to clear and mark pre-designated fields, so that the gliders bringing in more troops, jeeps, and anti-tank guns could land safely. The gliders were due in at about 0300.

Major General Maxwell Taylor, Commander of the 101st Airborne.

Only one regiment of the 82nd Airborne Division, the 505th PIR (Parachute Infantry Regiment), landed roughly where it was supposed to. The other two regiments, the 507th and 508th PIR, landed in the swampy flooded ground of the Merderet. Many men drowned. So heavily weighed down were they with equipment that some perished in less than two feet of water. The majority of the 82nd were fighting small but crucial actions where they landed. For these paratroopers, with their minds on survival, getting out of the flooded fields and onto terra firma was paramount. The embankment of the Cherbourg-Carentan railway was the best bet to lead to safety. Among the men headed for the embankment was Brigadier General Gavin, the 82nd's assistant commander, who at this time was busy trying to salvage some much-needed equipment from the swamps, along with a few lost men. Finding more men, General Gavin began to get them organized and marched them south along the railway embankment to seize his objectives – the bridges over the Merderet. All around them was heavy fighting, for they had come down virtually in the middle of the German 91st Airlanding Division.

EYEWITNESS

The Germans were all around us, of course, sometimes within 500 yards of my command post, but in the fierce and confused fighting that was going on all about they did not launch the strong attack that could have wiped out our eggshell perimeter defenses.
General Matthew B. Ridgway, commander, 82nd Airborne Division

The 505th PIR had landed northwest of St Mère Église. This had been through the sheer determination of their pilots. Their mission was to seize and hold the vital crossroads of the town. At about 0100 that day, the inhabitants of St Mère Église were busy fighting a house fire on the side of the town square. It was thought to have been started by a stray incendiary bomb or tracer bullet. The fire was getting out of hand and the small fire brigade could not cope. The mayor rushed to the German headquarters to see if he could get the curfew lifted so as to get as many volunteers as possible to form a bucket chain. The Germans

Major General Matthew Ridgway and Brigadier General James Gavin, commander and deputy commander of the 82nd Airborne.

agreed and turned out the guard to supervise the townsfolk. The church bell was ringing loudly, but above all the commotion, aircraft engines could be heard approaching from the west. It was not long before anti-aircraft batteries around the town were adding their own noise to the now deafening din. Parachutes were spotted floating down. This was a stick from the 506th PIR of the 101st Airborne Division, who were supposed to be landing about seven miles away. These men dropped in and around the town. Four were killed immediately, riddled by German bullets as they tried to free themselves from their harnesses. The remainder scattered.

Lieutenant Charles Santarsiero of the 506th PIR was standing in the door of his plane as it passed over St Mère Église, "We were about four hundred feet up, and I could see fires burning and Krauts running about. There seemed to be total confusion on the ground. All hell broken loose. Flak and small-arms fire was coming up and those poor guys were caught right in the middle of it."

About fifteen minutes later a platoon from the Fox Company of the 505th PIR landed directly in the town, right in the middle of the now fully alerted German garrison. One soldier floated down into the blazing building and the explosives he was carrying blew up; others came down in the square itself or got snagged up in the trees surrounding it. They were immediately shot. The mayor, Alexandre Renaud, remembers standing in the square when a paratrooper plunged into a tree. Almost immediately, as he tried frantically to get out of his

harness, he was spotted. "About half a dozen Germans emptied the magazines of their sub-machine guns into him and the boy hung there with his eyes open, as though looking down at his own bullet holes."

One man, Private John Steele, had his parachute catch on the steeple of the church and he just hung there unable to move. On the way down something hit him that felt "like the bite of a sharp knife." He had been shot through the foot. He hung there feigning death. The noise of the church bells alongside his head temporarily deafened him. Finally he was saved by a German observer stationed in the belfry.

Private First Class Ernest Blanchard heard the church bell ringing and saw the enemy bullets passing all around him. The next minute he watched, horrified, as a man floating down almost beside him "exploded and completely disintegrated before my eyes." No doubt this was caused by the explosives the man was carrying. The majority of the 3rd Battalion, 505th PIR, rallied and slipped into the now relatively quiet town, which the Americans captured, thanks to a panic flight by the conscripted Austrian soldiers who were occupying it.

It was now 0430 hours on June 6th. Lieutenant Colonel Krause of the 3rd Battalion pulled a battered Stars and Stripes from his pocket, went over to the town hall, and ran it up the flagpole. It was the very same flag that the battalion had hoisted over Naples.

St Mère Église became the first French town liberated by the Americans. Now the 1st Battalion of the 505th PIR set out to capture and hold the bridges over the Merderet at La Fière and Chef-du-Pont, while the 2nd Battalion was to establish a blocking line to the north.

Lieutenant Colonel Vandervoort, commander of the 2nd Battalion, had broken his ankle on landing. (On the whole, however, the battalion had had a comparatively good landing. Its pathfinders had marked their drop zone exactly, and the majority of the men had come down within it). Vandervoort laced his combat boot tighter and began using his rifle as a crutch. In a very short space of time he had gathered about 600 men. None of the other units dropped that night could boast of such an achievement. Starting out for their objective, Neuville-au-Plain, Vandervoort caught sight of two men pulling an ammunition cart. They were quickly, if grudgingly, commandeered as chauffeurs.

Meanwhile, the 101st Airborne had a more difficult landing to achieve, for if they overshot their drop zones they would risk landing in the flooded area behind Utah Beach, or, worse still, in the sea. If they landed too short they would come down in the area of operations of the 82nd Airborne Division. In all, the landing was a complete mess with the men scattered like chaff.

Captain Charles G. Shettle jumped near the village of Angoville-au-Plain, just north of Carentan. He blew up a vital German communications line, and then, with about twenty men, the best he could muster in the darkness, he marched to the north bridge near Le Port reaching it at 0400. Shettle's tiny command tried to cross the second bridge and seize a foothold on the other side, but the Germans counter-attacked and forced the small band of paratroopers back onto the northern side.

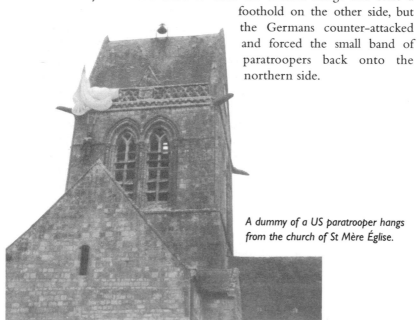

A dummy of a US paratrooper hangs from the church of St Mère Église.

Colonel Johnson's 501st PIR, was about to jump from his plane, the green light was on, when suddenly a bale of supplies fell in front of the door blocking his exit. When they got it clear and finally jumped, the force of 150 men landed just north of their objective, right where they wanted to be, at the locks at La Barquette. The green light had

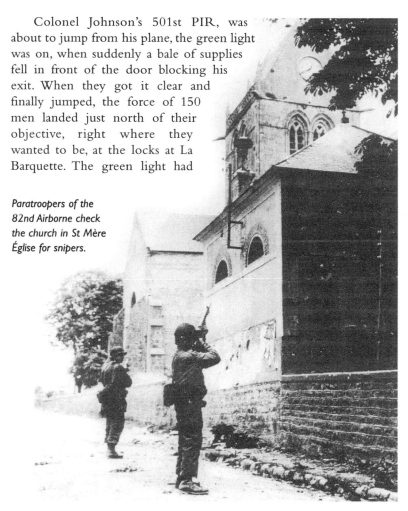

Paratroopers of the 82nd Airborne check the church in St Mère Église for snipers.

come on prematurely! The lucky troopers seized the locks, which controlled the flood waters in the area, without a fight.

The 506th PIR had the task of securing Exits One and Two from Utah Beach, plus capturing the two bridges that spanned the Douve. Colonel Sink, commander of the 506th PIR, landed west of Sainte Marie-du-Mont and, with about forty of his men, linked up with the 1st Battalion of his regiment, which had landed nearby. He established his command post at the small hamlet of Caloville. Not far away at

Paratroopers of the 101st Airborne show off their trophies.

Hiesville, Lieutenant Colonel Ewell of the 501st PIR was setting up a command post for the 1st Division.

At a little after 0600 the decision was made to attack and capture Exit One from Utah, to help the troops coming in from the sea. Their attack began at Pouppeville with only forty men. The village was heavily defended by men from the German 91st Airlanding Division and it took the small American force over three hours of determined house-to-house fighting to finally overcome the garrison. With Pouppeville in American hands so was Exit One. The US 4th Division coming into Utah first made contact with the 101st Airborne Division here on Exit One at a little after 1100 on June 6th.

The 502nd PIR was responsible for the two northern exits from Utah. Lieutenant Colonel Cole, commander of its 3rd Battalion, had landed not far from St Mère Église. He had spent the night making his way toward the objectives, picking up stragglers on the way. By dawn he had a force of about seventy-five men, mostly from his own battalion, but also some from the 82nd Airborne Division, and was heading toward St Martin-De-Varreville. After a slight brush with a German patrol, he reached the enemy battery there.

The Germans had set up a mobile gun position on the outskirts of the village, which they kept switching about to avoid Allied bombing. The village itself was damaged and deserted. Cole split his group and sent each half to seize Exits Three and Four. Near Audouville-la-Hubert the Americans could see large numbers of enemy troops retreating from Utah Beach across the causeway. By 0930 the Allies were slaughtering the Germans. By midday both exits were safely in American hands.

Many acts of heroism took place in the early hours of June 6th, too many to mention, but one in particular must be told. Another objective of the 502nd PIR was a large group of buildings being used as a barracks by one of the coastal artillery batteries. It was about a mile inland from St Martin-de-Varreville. Sergeant Harrison Summers, with about fifteen reluctant men, was sent to secure the barracks. He set about it with a vengeance. Kicking in the door of the first building he sprayed the interior with bullets from his Thompson machine gun. Four Germans fell dead. The rest vanished out the back door. Looking around for support, and seeing the rest of his men hiding, Sergeant Summers went on to the next building. In he went shooting and out came more fleeing Germans. He gave a third building the same treatment, this time with covering fire from some of his shy comrades, for by now the Germans were awakening to the fact that they were under attack. On and on he went until finally one of his men joined him. Two buildings to go. In Summers went again. To his surprise, a group of German artillerymen was sitting down eating breakfast, oblivious to what was going on.

With no compunction Summers mowed then down. Finally, he came to the last and largest building, which had alongside it a shed and haystack. One of Summer's group fired tracers and set the shed and haystack alight. (The shed was being used as a stowage for ammunition and very soon exploded). At this point, a large party of Germans ran out and were either killed on the spot or fled. Some of the enemy artillerymen were now returning fire from the ground floor. Another American arrived with a bazooka. With one well-aimed shot he set the roof of that building on fire. As the fire intensified, the Germans ran out and again faced a hail of lead. Mission accomplished, Summers slumped to the ground and lit a cigarette, feeling "not very good," as he put it.

In the meantime, the American glider force had approached the peninsula from the same direction as the American paratroopers. The Americans preferred using the Waco Glider, which was smaller than its British counterpart, the Horsa, and not so heavy or prone to splintering on impact. The Waco was made of canvas and plywood on a tubular steel

A Douglas C-47 "Skytrain" about to snatch-lift a Waco glider. France, June, 1944

frame and was much easier to land in small fields; it could carry fifteen men or a small vehicle. Once released from the tow aircraft, and with its elementary controls, it would go into a steep dive as it approached the ground.

At 0330 the aircraft dropped to an altitude of about 160 meters and continued at that height to the landing zone. It was an uneventful trip, until about halfway across the twenty–two mile peninsula, when the German gunners opened up. From there on in, tracers filled the sky. Many men described the multi-colored flak arching into the sky around them as "the biggest fireworks display ever." Gliders at that height were also taking small arms hits which, according to Lieutenant Colonel Michael C. Murphy, who was the most senior pilot and flew the No. 1

lead glider, "Sounded like popcorn popping when the slugs passed through the fabric." It was later discovered that the No. 2 glider had taken ninety-one hits in the tail section alone!

In Murphy's glider was Brigadier General Don Pratt, assistant divisional commander of the 101st, and his jeep. He was not jump qualified and was supposed to be coming ashore with the remainder of the division on Utah Beach. However, he had arranged with General Taylor to go in by glider instead, so as to get into the battle quicker. Pratt's aide, who carried top secret documents and maps, flew with them as well. As a precaution, because of its "precious load," glider No. 1, nicknamed "The Flying Falcon," had been secretly armored. This of course made the machine much heavier than it should have been.

Just west of the landing zone, near the little town of Hiesville, Murphy saw the release signal, a green light shining from the plexiglas dome of the tow aircraft. He hit the release knob and heaved a sigh of relief. It had been hard work keeping the glider on a level course for over two hours.

A fully loaded CG-4A Waco glider touching down at seventy miles per hour could normally be stopped in 200-300 feet but, because of the extra weight it carried, No. 1 came down at over eighty miles per hour. To make matters worse, the ground was slick with dew. Murphy immediately stood on the brakes, but to no avail. The glider carried on for an extra two hundred feet before crashing into a hedgerow. General Pratt died instantly, his neck broken. Murphy suffered two broken legs, but still managed to crawl out, brandishing his pistol. His co-pilot was dead. Lieutenant May, the general's aide, was stunned but unhurt. General Don Pratt became the first general to die that day.

The fields and hedgerows of Normandy, known as the Bocage, were more of a hazard to the gliders than were the Germans. Pilots were not expecting banks of earth four to five feet tall topped with a thick impenetrable hedge. The fields were smaller and the trees taller than they had trained for in England. Many gliders slithered out of control in the wet grass and ended up crashing into these deadly banks. Others hit tree tops and the roofs of buildings, spewing out their cargo of men. Over 300 men became casualties. The men that survived, rallied and linked up with the paratroopers; the anti-tank guns and equipment salvaged from the gliders was to become invaluable.

EYEWITNESS

We could hear the sounds of planes in the distance, then no sounds at all. This was followed by a series of swishing noises. Adding to the swelling crescendo of sounds was the tearing of branches and trees followed by loud crashes and intermittent screams. The gliders were coming in rapidly, one after the other, from all different directions. Many overshot the field and landed in the surrounding woods, while others crashed into nearby farmhouses and stone walls.

In a moment, the field was complete chaos. Equipment broke away and catapulted as it hit the ground, plowing up huge mounds of earth.

Bodies and bundles were thrown all along the length of the field. Some of the glider troopers were impaled by the splintering wood of the fragile plywood gliders.

Private John Fitzgerald, 502nd PIR, 101st Airborne Division

At this point, the men of the two airborne divisions scattered widely over the Cotentin Peninsula that morning, heard a new sound. It was the sustained rumbling of a terrific bombardment coming from the coast, the prelude to the seaborne invasion.

Despite the bedlam and disorganization, the 82nd and the 101st had achieved much more than the average trooper could imagine sitting in his hole, or crouching behind a Norman stone wall. The airborne divisions had taken and secured their primary objectives, perhaps not in such great force as their commanders might have wished, but nevertheless, with sheer guts and determination small groups acting on their own initiative had done what they set out to do. In a way the scattering of their units had helped them. The Germans could see no set plan, no definite drop area that would give them a clue as to where the invasion was going to take place. With the help of the dummy parachutists (codenamed "Ruperts"), the enemy had been thrown into total bewilderment.

Also, unfortunately for the German 91st Airlanding Division, their commander, Lieutenant General Wilhelm Falley, was ambushed and killed by American paratroopers. He was rushing back to his headquarters after taking part in war game exercises in Rennes. Ironically, the games were concerned with how to repel an invasion.

The ambushing of General Falley was reported to General Ridgway, to which he replied:

Well, in our present situation, killing divisional commanders does not strike me as being particularly hilarious.
General Matthew Ridgway, commander, 82nd Airborne Division

By morning, the 101st Airborne had secured most of the causeways leading inland from Utah Beach, and had thrown up a hasty defense line on the southern flank, guarding against counter-attacks from the direction of Carentan. The 82nd Airborne had had a disastrous drop in the flooded area of the Merderet and Douve valleys. The flooding was far more extensive than the allies had thought. What looked like solid

A patrol from the 82nd Airborne in the streets of St Mère Église. Two troopers have found an alternative means of transport.

55

ground in aerial photographs actually turned out to be water with high grasses growing out of it. Despite not being able to capture or blow the bridges over the Douve nor to secure the west bank of the Merderet, the 82nd had nevertheless gone on to create chaos throughout the enemy positions. Their primary objective, St Mère Église, had in fact been taken and held. All through the day the Germans counter-attacked the town, desperate to reclaim it, but the paratroopers defended it stubbornly, often against overwhelming odds.

Soon the infantry from the beaches would be with them to relieve the pressure. The airborne story continues when they link up with the seaborne infantry and together fight for the liberation of the Cherbourg Peninsula.

CIRCUIT TWO

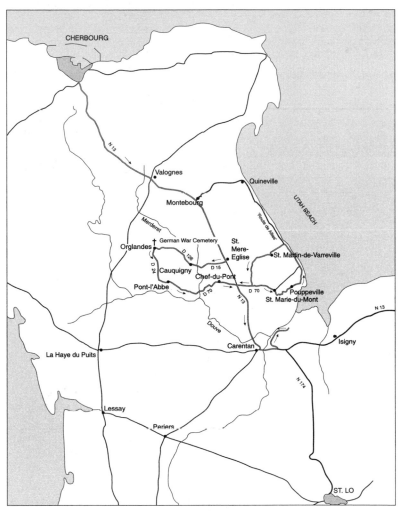

Circuit two. Cherbourg – St Mère Église – Oglandes – Sainte Marie-du-Mont – Cherbourg

From Cherbourg take the main road south (N-13); this will be signposted Valognes, Carentan, and St Lô. Sixteen kilometers south of Valognes take the turning signposted for St Mère Église. Drive into the center, where there is ample free parking in and around the town square. The church, in the center of the square, has a model of a parachutist hanging from the stone buttress throughout the summer months. This is the place where Private John Steele landed in the early hours of D-Day. Standing opposite the church is the Musée des Troupes Aéroportées [Airborne Troops Museum]. This is built on the site of the burning house where one of the paratroopers landed during the

The Route of Liberty begins at kilometer 0 St Mère Église or (right) at kilometer 00 Utah Beach.

massacre in the square. General Gavin laid the first stone for this superb museum on June 6th, 1961. The museum houses many exhibits contributed not only by local people but also by veterans from the 82nd and 101st Airborne Divisions. Pride of place in the two buildings that make up the museum are a Douglas C-47 transport plane and a fully restored Waco glider.

Also in St Mère Église, in front of the Mairie [Town Hall], is the marker stone for Kilometer 0. This is the first in a number of stones that retrace the "Voie de la Liberté" [Road of Liberty]. Kilometer 0 marks the start of the trail (since St Mère Église was the first town to be liberated by the Americans on D-Day). The trail is marked all the way from St Mère Église through France, Luxembourg, and into Belgium until it finishes at Bastogne. Stones are also located on the roads running north to Cherbourg which was liberated at the end of June, and east to Utah Beach where the Kilometer 00 stone marks the site of the first seaborne landings by Allied troops.

A walk around the square will reveal different plaques on trees and walls dedicated to the paratroopers landed or who were killed nearby. There are plenty of cafés and souvenir shops in the town center, as well as a US Army surplus store that will be of interest to the Battlefield Tourist. The shop fronts often have displays that change periodically and sometimes include photographs of visiting veterans. Also in the square is one of the eleven stones erected by the Comité du Debarquement. The church itself is also worth a visit, for inside there are two beautiful stained glass windows that have been dedicated to the American Airborne troops that liberated St Mère Église.

It is very difficult to organize a tour around the drop zones, since the paratroopers were so scattered (in fact the area in which they landed would cover over 180 square miles). Also, today, there is very little to see. What we can do, though, is take the Battlefield Tourist around the

59

various villages within the area, so that they can get an idea of what the countryside was like for the soldiers who fought there.

Most of the towns and villages in the area were liberated within a few days of D–Day by the combined efforts of the paratroopers and the seaborne troops that came ashore at Utah Beach. So we will mention some of these places in the chapter on Utah Beach (see Chapter 3).

From St. Mère Église head west and cross under the N-13, taking the country road marked D-15. This road will also cross the Cherbourg-Carentan railroad and the River Merderet. Back in 1944 this whole area had been extensively flooded. When you reach the hamlet of Cauquigny turn right onto the D-126 for Amfreville. The American pathfinders had trouble marking the drop zones north of here and, consequently, many men overshot and landed in the flooded marshes. Some drowned, weighed down by their equipment, while those that survived were forced to fight alone in the waterlogged fields until they could join up with their own, or other, units. The railroad, which was above the waterline of the floods, helped some of the lost troops get their bearings as they struggled to reform.

General Gavin had jumped east of Amfreville along with elements of the 507th PIR. Most of the 508th PIR jumped further to the south, around Gueutteville, and the 505th PIR jumped to the east between Amfreville and St Mère Église.

Continue along the D-126 through Gourbesville and turn right, onto the D-24, at the village of Orglandes. After leaving the village, on the left hand side, there is Orglandes German Cemetery. There are five German cemeteries in Normandy, in which are buried the remains of some 70,000 Axis servicemen killed in the battle for Normandy. The Orglandes was originally an American cemetery started as the Americans fought their way toward Cherbourg. The Americans later exhumed their dead and either concentrated the bodies in one of the two American cemeteries, at Saint James and Colleville–sur–Mer, or repatriated them to the US. In total some 14,000 American servicemen were flown back to the US at the government's expense. It was then that this area was taken over by the German Volksbund [a German peoples' association] who started the German cemetery in 1956. Completed in 1961, Orglandes cemetery is now the final resting place of some 10,152 German servicemen.

Drive back along the D-24. After five kilometers turn left onto the D-15 and drive through Pont-l'Abbé. Continue on the D-70 to Chef-du-Pont. Continue along the D-70, crossing under the railroad and N-13, toward Sainte Marie-du-Mont.

Looking right along this road toward the hamlet of Hiesville is the landing zone where many of the gliders of the 101st Airborne came down. Colonel Sink landed just west of here and established his command post at Caloville, a hamlet between Sainte Marie-du-Mont and Hiesville. This was also the area where Colonel Ewell of the 3rd Battalion, 501st PIR established the first divisional command post. Drive into Sainte Marie-du-Mont and turn right onto the road that circles the church. The Germans held onto the village until late in the afternoon of D-Day but were eventually forced to withdraw when the Americans brought up armored support from the 4th Infantry Division that had landed on Utah Beach.

Take the second turning opposite the church and follow the D-424 to l'Église. Turn left onto the D-329 and left again onto the D-115. Take the next right back onto the D-329 and drive into Pouppeville. This is where the paratroopers made the first contact with the seaborne forces. Continue through Pouppeville, on the D-329 and follow the road until you reach the Utah Beach Museum (see Chapter 3). You will notice that all the roads in this area have been named in honor of soldiers who landed on June 6th, 1944.

Drive along the D-421 coast road named "Route des Allies," heading north toward the Varreville dunes where it was planned that the first waves of combat troop and DD (duplex drive) tanks would come ashore onto Utah Beach. You can still see evidence of the excellent construction of the German bunkers along the sea front. Despite a heavy naval and aerial bombardment prior to the invasion, many of these bunkers remained intact on D-Day. Fortunately, the landings took place further south, next to where the Utah Beach Museum is now situated, and so avoided the heavily fortified positions along this part of the coast.

Take a left turn onto the D-423 and drive into St Martin-de-Varreville. It was here that the Germans had a mobile battery which, on May 29th, was bombed with great accuracy by the RAF. Lieutenant Colonel Cole, having landed near St Mère Église, mustered his men and marched on this village, which was one of his objectives. He found the battery empty and went on to secure the area and the beach Exits Three and Four near Audouville-la-Hubert, where they were finally able to link up with the seaborne troops of the 4th US Infantry Division.

Drive along the D-423, straight on at the crossroads with the D-115, and onto the D-129. Turn right onto the D-70 and join the southbound carriageway, on the N-13, to Carentan. From Carentan head northeast toward Brévands and the hamlet of Le Port. From Le Port follow the road that runs parallel to the River Douve, down toward La Barquette. Along this part of the river were the two bridges that were the objective of the 3rd Battalion, 506th PIR. Further along, at La Barquette, the 1st and 2nd Battalion of Colonel Johnstone's 501st PIR were tasked with the capture of the lock gates and with blowing the bridges on the main Carentan–Cherbourg highway and railroad.

From La Barquette you can make your way into Carentan or else rejoin the N-13 and head north to St Mère Église or Cherbourg.

3

UTAH BEACH TO CHERBOURG

THE US 4TH INFANTRY DIVISION under the command of Major General Raymond O. Barton was to land on the eastern side of the Cotentin peninsula. The beach area was codenamed Utah, and subdivided into Uncle and Victor sections. It was situated immediately in front of Les Dunes de Varreville, between beach Exits Three and Four.

The landings had been planned to the very last detail. DD (duplex drive) Sherman tanks, fitted with propellers and designed to float in water (see Chapter 5) would land at exactly 0630 after swimming in from five kilometres. The tanks would be at the low tide water's edge when the naval bombardment ceased, and the specially-equipped landing craft, fitted with hundreds of rockets, had fired. Close behind the DD tanks would come the first wave assault troops, the 2nd Battalion of the 8th Infantry Regiment (IR). These would be brought in by Landing Craft Vehicle Personnel (LCVP), also known as "Higgins" boats, after the craft designer. There would be twenty of these craft in the first wave, each carrying approximately thirty fully-equipped men. Five minutes later the second wave carrying the 1st Battalion, 8th Infantry, combat engineers and demolition teams would land, closely followed by more Landing Craft Tanks (LCTs) bringing in tank dozers and fighting tanks.

That was the plan – but it didn't work out quite so smoothly. The most crucial disaster of the landing happened when three out of the four Control Guide boats hit mines and sank. This caused the LCTs to mill around aimlessly. Without a guide they could not go in. One of the LCTs hit another mine and immediately sank, taking its precious cargo of four tanks with it. The last surviving Control boat, realizing what had gone wrong, rounded up the LCTs and started to lead them in. To make up for precious time lost, the Guide boat took the LCTs nearer to the beach to launch their DD tanks. In fact, two kilometres nearer. The strong current and the confusion of smoke and explosions led to the Control boat to slide south of its intended launching zone. Three kilometers from the beach, the ramps of the LCTs went down and out trundled the DD tanks to begin their slow approach to the shore. Most of the men in the landing craft were so seasick they hardly cared what happened to them. Anything was better than being tossed about in the flat-bottomed Higgins boats.

EYEWITNESS

That guy Higgins ain't got nothing to be proud of about inventing this goddamned boat.
Unidentified GI, 4th Infantry Division

On the way in, the landing craft passed bodies floating in the water. Some were shouting for help, others were dead. Those who dared to raise their heads above the sides of their landing craft witnessed the horrors for themselves. A few did. One was overheard passing comment:

EYEWITNESS

Them lucky bastards — they ain't seasick no more.
Unidentified GI, 4th Infantry Division

Because of the time delay, the first wave infantry was now hot on the heels of the tanks, so much so that they overtook the tanks and actually landed ahead of them. Five hundred yards from the beach a couple of designated landing craft sent up smoke signals, a sign for the navy to stop the shelling. The moment of truth was upon the men packed into the landing craft. Easy Company of the 2nd Battalion of the 8th IR stormed ashore and became the first Allied company of the entire

Troops from the 4th Infantry Division coming ashore at Utah Beach.

invasion force to hit the beaches of Normandy.

Prior to the landings, medium bombers of the 9th Air Force had saturated the area with bombs. The navy had added its own fair share of high explosive from the likes of the battleship *USS Nevada*. Also thousands of rockets had been blasted into the area by the Landing Craft Tank Rockets (LCTRs). It was little wonder that not much opposition awaited the American landing. Most Germans on that particular stretch of beach had either fled, were too shaken to do anything, or were already dead.

The landing craft could not give the men of the 2nd Battalion a dry landing. A sand bar about 100 yards out stopped the LCVPs from getting any closer to shore. They had no choice but to let down their ramps and off-load the troops. Waist deep in water, the soldiers waded to the beach, glad to reach dry land again after their ordeal.

The tide was a long way out. Confronting the soldiers once they got

to dry sand was about 500 meters of gently sloping beach, strewn with obstacles. Beyond that lay a belt, approximately 100 meters wide, of low sand dunes. Intermittent rifle fire from the few Germans who remained was all the soldiers of the 8th IR had to contend with during the initial landing.

The men rushed forward into the dunes and took cover behind the four-foot concrete sea wall. Their officers, conferring with one another, soon realized this was not the area of the landing beach they had been briefed about. The sand models back in England bore no resemblance to what they were now seeing. Looking behind them toward the sea, they noted that the second wave was already landing, but slightly to the right of where they themselves had just come in. Tanks on the beach were immediately engaging the enemy strongpoints that had remained functional.

The German fortified position at this spot was called W-5. Oberleutnant Jahnke was the officer in charge. He, and what men remained, started to pour fire down onto the shore line. One of the armaments under Jahnke's command was an old French Renault tank dug into the dunes. This started firing but was soon put out of action by a well-aimed 75mm shell from one of the Sherman tanks coming up the beach. Jahnke had been amazed to see the tanks swimming toward him. He decided to combat this threat with his own secret weapon – small, remote-control tanks packed with explosives. These weapons, called "Goliaths," could be guided toward the American tanks and detonated when close by. Unfortunately for Jahnke, the heavy bombardment had upset the delicate mechanisms of the Goliaths and they would not work.

American soldiers started piling up on the beach as the engineers and demolition teams continued with the dangerous task of blowing up and clearing the beach obstacles. This job was particularly difficult because the soldiers landing on the beach were using the beach defenses as cover from the German fire. An exit had to be found to relieve the congestion.

Brigadier General Theodore Roosevelt, Jr., eldest son of former President Teddy Roosevelt (and a cousin of Franklin D. Roosevelt), was in the first wave. He was not a healthy man, having already had a heart attack and suffering from arthritis. Despite his failing health he had pleaded with General Barton to let him go in with his troops as it would "steady the boys" as he put it. Reluctantly Barton agreed, and so Roosevelt was seen strutting up and down the beach with his cane encouraging his men as they exited their landing craft. He hated helmets, so he only wore a

US Cemetery, Omaha Beach.

knitted cap, seemingly oblivious to the danger all around him.

Roosevelt had already been up to the sand dunes and conferred with his officers there, agreeing that they had landed about one mile south of their designated landing area. He also realized that strongpoint W-5 was holding up the advancing troops and must be eliminated in order to open an exit. At this time a German battery to the north in the region of Les-Dunes-de-Varreville began to zero in on the beach area. High explosive shells from German 88s rained down on Utah Beach, blowing huge craters in the sand. Men went to ground or hid behind the stationary tanks. One unit of GIs, with tanks in support, charged toward W-5 and, after a brief fight, overwhelmed it. The exit leading to Sainte Marie-du-Mont was open. Oberleutnant Jahnke was pulled out of the sand by a GI and sent to a temporary prisoner holding area on the beach. While there, Jahnke was wounded by one of the German shells landing on the beach. Meanwhile, the engineers blew holes in the sea wall and the bottleneck was broken. Vehicles and men began to roll inland.

Roosevelt and his staff now faced a different dilemma. Should they move the entire landing force north to meet with the original plan, or should they drive directly inland using Exits One and Two immediately in front of them. Roosevelt made the decision to go inland right where he was and with the immortal words, "We'll start the war from right here," he got things moving. It was a wise move and a lucky error. As it happened, the Germans had a much stronger fortification at the site of the

GIs of the 4th Infantry Division greet civilians as they pass through Sainte Marie-du-Mont.

original beach area. By chance, Roosevelt's part of the 4th Infantry Division had landed in a relatively quiet sector. Reports from units coming ashore at the planned landing ground confirmed that the opposition there was strong.

Tanks from the 70th Tank Battalion were now nosing up and down the beach looking for an exit through the sea wall. They found one the engineers had blown open, and moved out onto the coast road immediately paralleling the dunes. One group of tanks went south and came to Exit One, which led to Pouppeville. Three tanks were disabled by mines, but now they were joined by infantry from the 2nd Battalion of the 8th IR, and carefully nosed forward across the causeway. The tanks, and the infantry supporting them, were taking light mortar fire and there was still the hazard of mines but they finally made the western side of the flooded area, just on the outskirts of Pouppeville.

They approached cautiously as no one from the 4th Division had any idea whether or not the paratroopers dropped in the early hours of the morning had succeeded in taking the village. Suddenly an orange flare shot up, and a group of US paratroopers stepped out into the open. It was 1110 hours and the 101st Airborne Division had met the 4th Infantry Division; the first major link up between the airborne and seaborne Allied troops on D-Day. Exit One was now officially opened. The units pushed on together, to take Sainte Marie-du-Mont. Meanwhile the men stumbling forward through the dunes were encountering anti–personnel mines, deadly devices that once stepped on shot up about waist-high and exploded, showering lethal ball bearings all around.

EYEWITNESS

Under the Command of General Eisenhower, Allied naval forces, supported by strong air forces, began landing Allied armies this morning on the northern coast of France.
Press Release, 0933 hours, June 6th 1944

By 1030, the 12th IR had followed in behind the 8th IR but the traffic from Exit Two had now ground to a standstill, absolutely jam-packed with vehicles. Occasionally German shellfire knocked out one of the trucks, causing it to block the causeway. The bulldozers were kept busy, pushing any disabled vehicles into the flooded land in order to keep the exit open.

In the meantime, the 1st Battalion, 8th IR, was trying to clear Exit Three. Getting impatient with the delay, the 12th IR decided it couldn't wait any longer and struck out across the flooded land in a northwesterly direction.

Shortly after midday the 22nd IR moved off Utah Beach to try to secure Exit Four – the final unsecured route inland. The 3rd Battalion of the 22nd moved north along the coast road, mopping up the coast fortifications as it went, and securing a flank for the whole division at the coastal village of Les Cruttes. The other two battalions of the 22nd, meanwhile, waded northwest through the floods, sometimes in water up to their chests. They reached dry land just short of St. Germain-de-Varreville, and by late afternoon had linked up with elements of the 82nd Airborne.

By midday vehicles and men were pouring ashore almost unmolested at Utah, save for a few sporadic explosions from German 88s. The real invasion was, in fact, going better than the training exercises in England. Casualties had been surprisingly light, mainly due to the error in landing and the heavy and highly accurate pre-invasion bombardment. Only 197 men had been killed or wounded on Utah. Sixty more were missing, believed drowned, probably when the LCT blew up and sank. The 4th Infantry Division had sustained more casualties at the rehearsals for the invasion on Slapton Sands, in England, back in May.

A little out to sea from Utah Beach are the islands of St Marcouf. A detachment of cavalry landed here anticipating that it would be heavily fortified. The area had to be made safe before any actual landings took place. By 0530 the cavalry had secured the island. It was totally deserted, but by the end of the day twenty men had been killed or wounded by mines that the Germans had planted there.

By mid–afternoon Utah Beach had been transformed into a hive of industry. Vehicles of every shape and form were streaming ashore and heading inland. Landing craft were
disgorging their precious cargoes of soldiers, rations, and petrol, and all the things needed to keep the momentum going. The engineers and Seabees (Combat Engineers from the US Navy) had cleared the majority of obstacles and all routes off the beach were now well and truly open. At the same time the wounded and the prisoners of war were being taken back to the waiting ships for transportation to England. By the end of the first day's fighting, the 4th Infantry Division had linked up with 82nd and 101st Airborne and secured the beachhead. The division was ready to take on its next objectives on the morning of June 7th.

By mid–morning the next day, the Americans had carved out an area

Soldiers of the 8th Infantry Regiment making their way through the flooded area behind Utah Beach.

behind the beach almost three miles in depth. The two airborne divisions occupied an area some twenty-five miles square but, within this area, isolated pockets of Germans were still resisting strongly.

Four battalions of tanks had been sent to St Mère Église to reinforce the hard-pressed elements of the 82nd Airborne there. The Germans would lose vast numbers of men during the fighting around the town. The 82nd Airborne, west of the River Merderet, was having a tough time of it. The Germans were continually counter-attacking, but time and again the paratroopers held their ground and forced them back. Casualties were high on both sides, and because of their isolated positions it was impossible for the wounded Americans to be evacuated.

The 4th Division moved north to try to capture the coastal batteries at Azeville and Sainte Marcouf (Crisbecq). These batteries still posed a threat to the men and materials flooding across the open

Right: A follow-up wave of apprehensive GIs head for the beach.

Below: A motorized column heads away from the beach up one of the now-clear draws.

beaches of Utah. They were formidable obstacles with solid concrete bunkers, and weapon emplacements protected by well dug-in German infantry. It was therefore decided to bypass the batteries for a while. To the south, the 101st Airborne firmly held on to the lock gates at La Barquette and to the bridges at Le Port, near Carentan, despite attacks by the young German paratroopers of von der Heydte's 6th Parachute Regiment.

On June 8th, the town of Sainte Come-du-Mont fell. This was the next village inland from Utah Beach, so it provided a jumping-off point for the attack on Carentan itself. All that separated the paratroopers from their prize were five bridges. Unfortunately, each side of the main road was flooded so the exposed road was the only route into the town. On June 10th, the 3rd Battalion, 502nd PIR, supported by artillery, attacked the Douve River bridges. It met stiff resistance on the outskirts of Carentan and suffered heavy casualties. The 1st Battalion passed through and pressed home the attack, also suffering heavy casualties. Finally, after two days of heavy fighting, the 502nd was withdrawn and the 506th PIR took their place. At the same time, men of the 327th Glider Regiment had already bypassed the town and were linking up with the troops who had come ashore at Omaha. These "Glider Riders" turned and attacked Carentan simultaneously from the east. Carentan fell after much bitter fighting late on June 12th with only isolated pockets of resistance to mop up. More importantly, after nearly a week of bloody fighting, the two beach heads at Utah and Omaha had finally been joined together.

The Germans did try a counter-attack using the 17th SS Panzer Grenadiers Division, but this attack was soon stopped by American P-47 "Thunderbolt" fighter planes and artillery bombardments. The Panzer Grenadiers suffered so much that they really didn't ever get back into the fight. Meanwhile the American paratroopers were fighting their opposite numbers, the German paratroopers, around the railway station in Carentan. By June 14th,

Troopers of the 101st Airborne in Carentan with a German prisoner.

Carentan was safely in American hands. The 101st Airborne Division were then given the task of protecting the southern flank of VII Corps and sealing off the base of the Cotentin peninsula, while the rest of the Corps moved on toward Cherbourg.

The Allies desperately needed a port of substantial size. General Montgomery had already made it clear that the two main objectives after landing would be Cherbourg and Caen, in order to secure ports.

The US 9th Infantry Division, which had landed on Utah on the

10th, was given the task of clearing the last strongpoint on the eastern coast, Quinéville. The village finally fell to the 9th Infantry Division on June 15th after intense fighting. By June 18th, the 4th Infantry Division had pushed the Germans back to a line north of Montebourg. Utah Beach was officially secure.

Meanwhile, the US 90th Infantry Division had been trying to push westward in the area of the Merderet river to aid the 82nd Airborne Division. The 90th had come up against tough opposition in its baptism of fire and had not made any substantial gains. Its commander was relieved by Montgomery because of the division's lack of toughness and aggressiveness.

The terrain was a nightmare for the attacking forces. The Norman Bocage country consisted of small fields surrounded by four-to five-foot earth banks, which were topped in turn by high and impenetrable hedges. In some places there was a double row of hedges separated by a drainage ditch. All these made ideal defensive positions. Despite this, the American advance cut off the peninsula by June 19th. Three American infantry divisions now turned north to march on Cherbourg while the 90th Division occupied the area from Barneville in the west, to Utah Beach in the east, safeguarding the southern flank of the units heading north.

Exit roads from Utah.

The 4th Infantry Division occupied Montebourg after it was bombed on the 19th while, to the west, the 9th Infantry Division captured Bricquebec. By the time the 4th Infantry Division reached Valognes on the 20th, the town was virtually unoccupied, confirming the fact that the remaining German forces on the peninsula were retreating northward and forming a strong defensive line around Cherbourg.

The German commander of that area, General von Schliebenand, had about 40,000 troops at his disposal. The nearer the GIs got to Cherbourg, the fiercer was the resistance. The terrain also changed, from the close knit fields of the Bocage to a more open countryside with a scattering of woodlands. The GIs met their first stubborn resistance on June 21st when they came up against well-emplaced troops sheltered in concrete bunkers.

A sniper behind every hedgerow – troops in the Bocage.

The fortifications were arranged in a semi-circle outside Cherbourg, stretching from Cap Lévi around to Branville.

The German's last major defense south of Cherbourg was Fort du Roule, which had been sufficiently armed and supplied to enable the defending force to hold out indefinitely. The French had fortified it before the German occupation and it had been improved by the Todt

General Wyche of the 79th Infantry with men of his division atop Fort du Roule.

engineering organization who modernized and strengthened it.

Before the 314th IR began its advance on this position, the Air Force attacked it with dive bombers. The 2nd Battalion captured the strongpoint, and in doing so Fox Company captured a motor pool containing large amounts of German material. Fox Company and Easy Company then stormed the fort itself and their action was such that the corps commander recommended that they be awarded unit citations. After a furious fight, the first white flag appeared at 1145 hours. The fighting was not over, however. One section had surrendered, but there were others who were willing to prolong the fight. Easy Company attempted to take some positions lower down within the fort, but was unable to do so, owing to fire from above and from the exposed left flank.

During this action Corporal John D. Kelly, of Easy Company of the 314th IR, won the 79th Division's first Medal of Honor. His platoon was inching up the fortress face when it was pinned down by enemy machine gun fire from a deeply entrenched strongpoint on the slope below the peak. The area was almost bare of natural cover. In a few moments casualties skyrocketed. The Medal of Honor citation takes up the story:

The US Navy stood off Cherbourg to keep the Germans from

Citation of Medal of Honor
Corporal John D. Kelly
Company "E,"
314th Infantry Regiment

Kelly volunteered to try to knock out the strongpoint. Arming himself with a pole charge about 10 feet long, with 15 pounds of TNT affixed, he climbed the slope under a withering blast of machine-gun fire and placed the charge at the strongpoint's base. The subsequent blast was ineffective, and again, alone and unhesitatingly, he braved the slope to repeat the operation. This second blast blew off the ends of the enemy guns. Corporal Kelly then climbed the slope a third time to place a pole charge at the strongpoint's rear entrance. When this had been blown open he hurled hand grenades inside the position, forcing survivors of the enemy gun crews to come out and surrender.

The US 79th Infantry Division in the Avenue du Paris, Cherbourg.

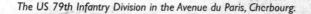

reinforcing their positions from the sea and were on call for any bombardment that the infantry might need – and the army was likely to need all the help it could get. Such was the ferocity of the fighting and the determination of the defenders that during one attack on the port, thirty-six Sherman tanks were knocked out in one go. On the night of June 21st, General Collins of VII Corps sent Schlieben an ultimatum saying it was useless to carry on as he was entirely surrounded. General Collins received no reply.

The air force launched a bombing raid on the main line of resistance that severely disrupted German organization and reduced their morale considerably. For the next two days, the 4th Infantry Division started mopping up the bunkers near the northern coast at Maupertus–sur–Mer; the 79th Infantry Division in the center was being held up at Hardinvast; the 9th Infantry on the left was mired down and not making any progress. Clearly, the capture of Cherbourg was going to be a long slow job.

By June 26th the lower levels of Fort du Roule had been neutralized. General Schlieben and his staff finally surrendered to the 9th Infantry Division, but not before the garrison commander made an unusual request to the Americans in order to keep his honor and dignity:

EYEWITNESS

I would be dishonored if I surrender. I could not resist an armored attack, for I have no more anti-tank guns, but I can resist against your infantry.
Generaloberst Schlieben, commander, Fort du Roule

The American officer moved ONE tank forward . . . and the Germans surrendered. Honor kept!

Several other areas still resisted but were eventually overcome until Cherbourg itself was finally captured on June 27th, 1944. Fighting stopped once and for all on July 1st and the northern Cotentin peninsula was in Allied hands. There to witness the liberation of the battered city was war correspondent McCardell:

EYEWITNESS

Rain was falling on our faces when we awakened. It was a cold, gray, misty dawn, the column was forming up in the mud for the final advance into Cherbourg. We moved forward into a deserted quarter of the city, evidently a section in which working people had lived. Concussion had shattered every window, every bit of glass. The telephone and electric light wires were broken tangles. But most of the buildings did not appear to have been damaged seriously by either the bombings or shellfire. The Germans had bricked up many windows and doors, leaving only narrow embrasures from which machine guns would sweep the street.
McCardell, war correspondent

The cost of capturing Cherbourg had been high, with VII Corps suffering 22,119 casualties. On the German side, 39,000 were taken prisoner and another 14,000 Germans were casualties. The Allies now had a firm grip in France; the Germans could have no hope of driving them back into the sea.

Unfortunately, the port the Allies had fought so hard to obtain was not immediately available. The Germans had had time to demolish the port area of Cherbourg and were convinced that it would take a very long time for the Allies to get it back into working order. In fact it took the Americans less than a month to repair the damage, and the first ships sailed in on July 16th. A few weeks later a huge drum was towed into the port. Coiled around the drum were the final stages of "PLUTO" (Pipe Line under the Ocean). There were four lines in all. When hooked up ashore, these lines would pump over 250,000 gallons of gasoline a day from the Isle of Wight to Cherbourg. It was in full operational use by August 12th and was also used to pump oil and water.

The next objective of the American army was to break out of the Cherbourg peninsula and head south. By the beginning of July, the GIs were ready to attack La Haye-du-Puits, Sainteny, and finally St Lô.

The countryside in this area was thick Bocage again; the roads were narrow sunken lanes. Once again, the terrain favored the defenders. Each hedgerow and ditch was a mini-fortress where a sniper might lie in wait, or a Panzer Faust [German anti-tank weapon, similar to the bazooka] might be waiting to knock out a vulnerable Sherman. Reaching the middle of a field was the point of no return!

La Haye-du-Puits was an important road junction surrounded by steep wooded heights. On July 3rd General Bradley threw all four divisions of the newly formed VIII Corps (the 90th and 79th Infantry Divisions and the 82nd and 101st Airborne Divisions) against this well-defended area. Capturing it would open an unimpeded passageway to the south. The Germans knew this only too well. They held on stubbornly and took terrible casualties; it was not until July 9th that the Americans finally subdued the town. A testament to the ferocity of the fighting for La Haye-du-Puits was later documented in the *Official History*.

It was in the La Haye-du-Puits that Lieutenant Arch B. Hoge, Jr., of Tennessee, raised the same small Confederate flag that had been raised by his uncle over a village in France in World War One, and which had been raised by his grandfather over a town in the United States during the Civil War.

At 0645, Company "K" was ordered to move out around the right flank of the Third Battalion and make a reconnaissance in force into La Haye du Puits. Despite stiff resistance it gained control of the railroad station on the northern outskirts of the town, but the Germans blasted away with everything they had and the company had to pull out. Then Division Artillery unveiled what GI witnesses hailed as "the prettiest damned precision artillery in this man's war." Lieutenant Colonel James B. "Kannonball" Kraft's 312th Field Artillery Battalion "paced" Lieutenant Colonel Olin E. "Tiger" Teague's First Battalion of the 314th Regiment to the very rim of the city's defense. A German artillery observation post in the city's cathedral lingered too long. A burst of artillery fire scored a direct hit on the church steeple and when the infantry entered the town hours later they found the German artillery observers sprawled in the public square.

Official History, US 79th Infantry Division

The capture of La Haye-du-Puits gave the weary attackers a momentary respite. Casualties on both sides were severe. The 79th Division had taken 2,930 casualties in eleven days of fighting. La Haye-du-Puits also proved to be the last action for the battle-weary airborne divisions who had borne the brunt of so much of the fighting in the Normandy Campaign. They were sent back to England on July 13th and 14th.

Next target for the advancing Americans was the town of Lessay. The town had earlier received German reinforcements in response to the Allies dropping dummy parachutists. The German had been deceived by the ruse and had rushed troops into the area as early as June 7th to combat what they thought was an invasion from the west. Now these troops of the German 84th Corps tried to stop the American offensive, but they were soon on the retreat. On July 27th the Americans entered a ruined town.

Meanwhile, the US VII Corps, which consisted of the 4th, 9th, and 83rd Infantry Divisions, was attacking further to the south. Their route would generally follow the Carentan-to-Périers highway. Either side of the road was thick with marshes and so would slow movement down.

An idea of the ferocity of the fighting by VII Corps is shown by the

83rd Infantry Division, which had been fought to a standstill just before the town of Sainteny. The 2nd SS Panzer (Das Reich) Division, hurriedly rushed from west of Caen, along with paratroopers from the 6th Parachute Regiment, completely stymied the American advance. The 83rd gained 200 meters and captured six prisoners, but lost 1,450 men in the process. The following day, hot on the heels of a tremendous barrage from VII Corps artillery, the division advanced another 1,500 meters but not withbout suffering more casualties.

Some medics, captured by the Das Reich Division, were sent back to the 83rd Infantry Division with a note saying that they were more needed by their own side, but that, if the fortunes of war changed, the Germans would be pleased to be offered their services.

The 4th Infantry Division came to the 83rd's aid, but even this well-seasoned, tough division could make little progress and also suffered many casualties. Eventually, on July 15th, VII Corps was pulled out of what was called "The Isthmus" to go and give support to the newly formed XIX Corps north of St Lô. Their area of operation was handed over to Middleton's VIII Corps.

CIRCUIT THREE

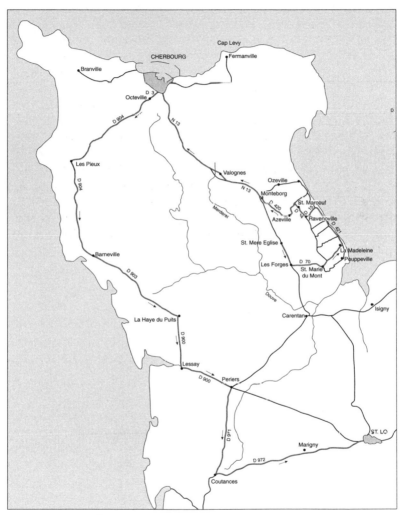

Circuit three: St Mère Église – Sainte Marcouf – Azeville – Cherbourg – Coutances – Cherbourg

FROM ST. MÈRE ÉGLISE DRIVE SOUTH on the N-13 to Les Forges, turn left on the D-70 to Sainte Marie-du-Mont. Pass through the small town still on the D-70 to arrive at La Madeleine. This is Utah Beach, the actual point where the US VII Corps landed on June 6th, 1944.

The German fortifications here made up the strongpoint W-5. The blockhouse on the left has been converted into a memorial crypt. On top of the bunker is a monument to the 1st US Engineer Brigade who landed here on June 6th. Also there is a memorial for the 90th Infantry Division. A German gun still faces out to sea. On the other side of the gap between the dunes is an excellent museum, which is housed in another part of the old W-5 fortifications. Outside the museum are positioned various artifacts of the landing, including a relatively new item, an LCVP, or Higgins Boat. There are also a few good examples of the type of beach obstacles Generalfeldmarschall Rommel had positioned along the Normandy beaches back in 1944. Sited near the museum is one of the markers of the "Liberty Way" at Kilometer 00.

The beach area is now as safe as the other beaches and gets packed with vacationers during the summer, though care should always be taken when exploring any of the sand dunes and hidden bunkers. The tide on Utah Beach goes out a long way, so expect a lengthy walk to reach the water's edge at low tide. Standing on top of the dunes and looking inland one can see the area behind the beach that was flooded during the war. It is still quite marshy even today.

There is ample parking near the beach and museum and all the usual facilities are available. A good viewing point above Utah Beach is on top of the bunker above the crypt, to the north of the museum, near the 1st US Engineer Brigade Memorial. Here is laid out, in the form of direction arrows, all the points of interest, including the positions of warships taken up for the bombardment.

Drive north, away from Utah Beach, on the D-421. Along this stretch of coastline you will be able to see the remnants of Hitler's Atlantic wall on both sides of the roadway. On your right, you will pass one of the monument signals raised by the Comité du Débarquement and a memorial to the French General Leclerc. Take a left turn at Grand Hameau des Dunes and head inland on the D-15. At Ravenoville take a right turn onto the D-14 and head north toward the gun batteries at Sainte Marcouf (Crisbecq) and Azeville. Both batteries are well signposted on this road.

The battery at Sainte Marcouf was called Crisbecq by the Americans because this village was nearest the battery's position. It was the only heavy battery in the area and had weapons that could provide covering fire along the whole length of Utah Beach. Only two bunkers out of four were completely built but these still housed four 210mm guns and had additional anti-aircraft guns in place in and around the battery perimeter. The battery had a compliment of about 290 men. From April 1944 right up to the day of the invasion the area was regularly bombed. By June 7th a battalion from the 4th Infantry Division was attacking the area but suffered many casualties because of the stiff resistance of the German defenders. The following day the 4th resumed the attack with the aid of naval gunfire, but was still repelled. The Americans therefore ended up bypassing the battery and on June 12th when patrols filtered into the area they found the battery deserted and were able to occupy it without a fight.

The second battery at Azeville housed four 105mm guns in casements that were next to houses on the edge of the village. The 22nd IR of the 4th Infantry Division rushed the battery on June 7th, but were thrown back with heavy casualties. They attacked again the next day but met the same fate. On June 9th, an attack with flamethrowers chanced to ignite the battery's ammunition store and the German commander, along with 169 of his men, no longer having anything to fight with, surrendered.

From Azeville drive northwest on the D-420 to Montebourg. Montebourg was virtually destroyed in twelve days of heavy fighting. The Germans finally burned the town before they retreated northward. It is now completely rebuilt. From Montebourg drive north on the N-13 to Valognes. This town was liberated on the night of June 20th/21st by the 79th Infantry Division, but only after it had been almost completely destroyed.

Continue north along the N-13 to Cherbourg. During the night of June 21st General Collins had his three divisions deployed around the outskirts of Cherbourg and sent the German commander an ultimatum. It went unanswered and so the systematic bombing of the fortification began at 0040 hours. During the night, the 9th Infantry Division, after much hard fighting, occupied the heights overlooking the town. Tourlaville to the east was captured by the 4th Division on June 24th. Finally the main fort of Le Roule was captured on June 25th. The fort now houses the Musée de la Liberation de Cherbourg.

From Cherbourg, a drive east to Fermanville, or west to Branville, would show evidence of the sort of fortifications the Allies had to contend with in the attack on Cherbourg. Otherwise, leave Cherbourg on the Octeville road D-3 and drive south, onto the D-904, toward Les Pieux. Over this village, on the night of June 5th/6th, flew the Dakota C-47 transport planes carrying the paratroopers on their way to the drop zones. Carry on south to Barneville. The first elements of the 60th Infantry Regiment entered the town at about 0500 on June 18th. The Germans counter-attacked in mid-morning but were driven back. By reaching this point the Americans had succeeded in cutting off the peninsula. On the outskirts of the town is a stone commemorating the feat. Carry on south from Barneville on the D-903 to the important crossroads town of La Haye-du-Puits. This was finally captured on July 8th after it had been virtually destroyed.

Now take the D-900 to Lessay. Here the Germans tried to repulse the American offensive, but failed and were driven back and forced to abandon the town. The ancient Abbey Church of Lessay, an early Roman building of great historical importance, was left in ruins. It has now been rebuilt.

Turn left at the main crossroads in Lessay onto the D-900 to Périers. This town, along with Lessay and St Lô, was one of the priority objectives of the Americans during those first few days of July 1944. All the approaches to these towns had been blocked by felled trees or mine fields as SS units and German paratroopers struggled to defend every possible piece of the ground. As a result, the Americans made little progress for nine days and sustained many casualties. It was little wonder they eventually gave up the idea of taking Périers. Midway between Périers and Carentan is the small town of Sainteny, considered to be the hardest hit community in the area. All of its cattle were killed during the fighting and the town itself was razed to the ground. American troops finally secured a small portion of the Périers – St Lô highway (D-900) and found Périers destroyed mostly by American artillery and bombing. In the center of Périers, turn south on the D-971 to Coutances approximately fifteen kilometers away. On July 27th the US 1st Infantry Division and 3rd Armored Division drove on Coutances from the direction of St Lô hoping to isolate the German 84th Corps. They were held off by two SS divisions for a time but the Germans were unable to stop two armored divisions attacking from the southward rampaging VIII Corps. Coutances was liberated in the afternoon of July 28th,1944.

4

OMAHA BEACH TO COBRA

AT 0251 ON JUNE 6TH, USS Ancon, headquarters ship for Admiral Hall and General Gerow, commander of V Corps, dropped anchor in the transport area twenty kilometers off Omaha Beach. The weather was not good; a strong wind was blowing from the northwest, whipping up the waves to a height of three or four feet. Breakers on the beach were also high, less than ideal for a landing.

The area selected for the V Corps landings was a slightly crescent-shaped beach about 7,000 meters in length, situated between the villages of Vierville and Colleville. Men landing there would have a large area of open sand covered with beach obstacles to negotiate before the beach turned to a shingle bank that was, in places, up to fifteen meters wide. The western half of the shingle backed up to a seawall; in the eastern half, the bank merged into low sand dunes. Running parallel to the beach was a paved road, which dwindled to little more than a track as it ran toward the eastern half of the beach area.

Behind the road, the level sand was interspersed with tall grasses and marshes. Dotted along this coast were a few summer villas, which had either been turned into fortifications or flattened to improve fields of fire. The sands then rose in steep bluffs up to sixty meters (200 feet) high and covered with rough grass, scrub, and low bushes.

The exits from the beach were by means of five small, narrow valleys. The Americans called these "draws," and gave each one a title: D-1 (Vierville); D-3 (Les Moulins); E-1 (St Laurent); and E-3 (Colleville). The fifth draw at the extreme eastern end of the beach was designated F-1; it showed potential, but was only a steep narrow track. Once atop the bluffs the land still sloped but gave the impression of standing on top of a plateau. Here were open fields and orchards stretching back for just under a mile to the blacktop road. This road (now the D-514) passed through the coastal villages and ran from Isigny through to Port-en-Bessin.

The Germans had spent a lot of time building defenses along this stretch of coast. At low tide obstacles exposed were "Element C" (a gate-like metal structure), steel hedgehogs, and large posts driven into the sand. Most of these structures had mines or explosives, strapped to them and were designed for, and quite capable of, wrecking landing craft.

Concertina wire was laid along the top of the sea wall and dunes, and the beach flats heavily mined. In addition, the Germans built strongpoints that were especially formidable in the areas of the exit points. Every part of the beach and sands could be covered by fire from machine guns, mortars, and rifles. There were also gun emplacements that covered the entire length of the beach, housing a host of different caliber guns. Special walls were built onto the sides of these emplacements to conceal the barrels and muzzle flashes from anyone out at sea.

There were no heavy batteries at Omaha, but approximately five kilometers away, on the cliffs at Pointe du Hoc, it was believed the Germans had a battery of six 155mm French guns. These could easily range on either Omaha or Utah Beach. According to Allied intelligence, the German 716th Division was manning these defenses and it was not rated as a very strong division. It was believed that the naval and air bombardment would incapacitate them.

A German strongpoint on Omaha Beach as it appears today.

V Corp's assault plan was for four regiments – two from the veteran US 1st Infantry Division reinforced with two from the as-yet-untried 29th Infantry Division – to land on Omaha Beach. The two regiments from the 1st Infantry were the 16th and 18th IRs. From the 29th Infantry Division came the 116th and 115th IRs. In addition there was also a Provisional Ranger Force, taken from the 2nd and 5th Ranger Battalions, plus tanks, artillery, and of course engineers. This constituted "Force O."

First ashore would be the DD tanks from the 741st and 743rd Tank Battalions. These would provide the infantry with covering fire from the water's edge. The tanks would be closely followed by the first wave Regimental Combat Teams consisting of the 116th IR, 16th IR, plus Engineers and Rangers. Hard on their heels would be the 18th Regimental Combat Team from the 1st Infantry Division and the 115th Regimental Combat Team of the 29th Infantry Division.

On D-Day plus 1, the plan called for the follow-up force ("Force B") to land. This included the two remaining regiments from each of the divisions: the 175th IR of the 29th infantry Division, the 26th IR of the 1st Infantry Division, and all of the 2nd Infantry Division. Their objectives were to open the draws to traffic, to secure a beachhead, and then to push inland toward Gaumont and St Lô.

Omaha Beach, for planning purposes, was split into sections. First it was cut in half, so that the 29th Infantry Division would land in the west and the 1st Infantry Division in the east. The beaches were then further subdivided from west to east and designated Charlie, Dog Green, Dog White, Dog Red, and Easy Green, for the 29th Infantry Division. The beaches for the 1st Infantry Division were designated Easy Red, Fox Green, and Fox Red.

From twelve miles out, in the first light of dawn on June 6th, the naval guns trained around to face the shore. The GIs were already aboard their LCVPs and LCAs and were making their way toward France. For some it would be a journey of nearly four hours before they reached the shore. The sea was rough and the men with their heavy equipment made the small landing craft sit even lower in the water. Spray and solid waves came over the side adding to the misery of already seasick men. And, as if they had not already enough to contend with, they now had to bale, some with their helmets, to keep the craft from sinking. Some though, were unable to do anything about their predicament. As the Rangers headed toward the shore a frantic message was overheard on the radio:

EYEWITNESS

This is LCA 860! . . . LCA 860! . . . We're sinking! . . . We're sinking! . . . My God, we're sunk!
Unidentified crewman, LCA 860

An LCT sinking off Omaha Beach, June 6th, 1944.

As the naval guns opened up at 0550, Lieutenant General Omar Bradley, commander of the 1st US Army Group, plugged his ears and watched through binoculars from the bridge of the flagship *USS Augusta*. Bombers flew overhead to drop their loads on the beach defenses below them. To the men storming ashore, it was reassuring; surely nothing could live through this fusillade of bomb and shell. Unfortunately though, the bombers could see nothing of their targets. The landing beaches were wreathed in smoke and dust. Fearful of dropping bombs on their own men, the bombers instead released their loads into the fields behind the German defenses.

Two or three miles out to sea, the DD tanks were launched. In the 1st Infantry Division's area, disaster struck. Of the thirty-two tanks allotted to them, twenty-seven went to the bottom of the sea, taking some of their crews with them. The rough seas had either ripped their buoyancy canvasses off or had swamped the "swimming tanks." In the 29th Infantry Division's area, the LCT crewmen saw what happened and decided to take their tanks directly onto the beach. Although these tanks did manage to get onto the beach they suffered badly from enemy artillery fire.

The first wave approached the beach. The troops landing on the eastern end of Omaha passed men helplessly floating on rafts or doing their best to keep afloat in the choppy seas. They were what was left of the doomed DD tanks that had sunk on the way in. Thousands of explosive rockets shot overhead, turning the whole shoreline into a mass of smoke, dust, and fire. The naval bombardment lifted, and still there was no sign of Germans anywhere.

The Germans were there all the same, safe in their bomb-proof shelters, untouched by the airforce and naval bombardments. The rockets fired onto their positions had fallen short and landed in the surf.

In addition to all these disasters, the Allies had not been informed that the second-rate German 716th Division, which had been defending this section of the coast, had now been reinforced by troops from the crack 352nd Infantry Division. The Germans could not believe their eyes as the landing craft came toward them. Each made a perfect target. 200 meters out all was still relatively quiet, then, just before touch down, the men in the landing craft heard machine gun and mortar fire. Even more worrying was the fact they could hear lead pinging around their craft, and see the huge fountains of water made by artillery and mortar explosions.

As the ramps went down it became wholesale slaughter. This was the signal the Germans had been waiting for. They poured machine-gun fire into the open mouths of the landing craft. Bodies piled up on the ramps. Men climbed over the sides of their craft, deciding to take their chances in the sea. The water was up to their waists and in some cases over their heads. Carrying heavy equipment, and with uneven footing, the going was tough. Many of them, who were not shot, drowned, unable to get their equipment off in time.

Very few of the LCVPs and LCAs carrying the infantry made dry landings. Most hit the sandbars some distance from the actual beach. For those who made it to the shore, they had to cross at least 200 meters of open beach before they reached the relative safety of the seawall. The first wave got nowhere. Men took cover as best they could, behind

Omaha Beach as it appeared on D-Day — and as it appears now.

obstacles or the few tanks that were ashore; others crawled in with the tide with just their heads raised above the water. Later it was found that some of them had made it simply by staggering across the beach, having been too exhausted to do anything else. The ones who sought cover behind the obstacles in the surf merely prolonged their agonies. It was the same story all along "Bloody Omaha" as it would later be called.

Due to a strong coastal current and high winds virtually all the craft arrived out of position and ended up east of their objectives. This especially upset the plan for the engineer and demolition teams. They were now faced with unfamiliar terrain and defenses, different from those they had been trained to clear.

Their task was of the utmost importance, but only about half of the sixteen teams made it to the shore and they were over ten minutes late as well. They had only been allocated thirty minutes in which to complete their tasks and the engineers were sitting ducks for the German defenders. The rubber boats packed with the engineers' explosives made excellent targets. In more than one instance direct hits were scored, touching off the prima cord and explosives, usually resulting in many deaths. Only six of the sixteen bulldozers reached the sand, and three of these were promptly put out of action by artillery. (With the exception of the DD tank, the Americans had decided not to use any AVRE tanks (see Chapter 5) to help them clear the beaches. This decision no doubt added to the price the infantry had to pay on Omaha Beach).

Despite this, the engineers found what equipment they could and began the task of clearing the beach defenses. By now they were also hampered by the quickly rising tide, which began to cover the beach obstacles. In addition troops were using the obstacles as shelter from the maelstrom of bullets. In fact, the engineers were unable to use one of their bulldozers because the infantry was using it as cover. One team managed to prepare a thirty-yard gap for blowing, and were just about to leave the vicinity and take cover, when an explosion, probably a mortar, hit the prima cord, touching off the explosives prematurely. The result killed or wounded nineteen engineers and many of the infantrymen nearby. Eventually the engineers managed to blow six complete gaps and partially clear a further three gaps.

Two of the clear paths through the beach defenses were in the 116th Infantry Division's area. Four more were in the Easy Red sector of the 1st Infantry Division. Due to the loss of equipment only one of these paths could be marked clearly for the following waves of landing craft. Consequently the benefits of the engineers' courage and sacrifice were lost when the incoming tide covered the unmarked gaps.

Only one group of the initial assault force came in where it was supposed to. This was Able Company of the 116th IR, 29th Infantry

Division. It landed right on target, immediately in front of the heavily defended Vierville draw on sector Dog Green. Within ten minutes it had taken 97% casualties.

EYEWITNESS

As the first men jumped, they crumpled and flopped into the water. Then order was lost. It seemed to the men that the only way to get ashore was to dive head first in and swim clear of the fire that was striking the boats. But, as they hit the water, their heavy equipment dragged them down and soon they were struggling to keep afloat. Some were hit in the water and wounded. Some drowned then and there . . . . But some moved safely through the bullet-fire to the sand and then, finding they could not hold there, went back into the water and used it as cover, only their heads sticking out. Those who survived kept moving forward with the tide, sheltering at times behind underwater obstacles and in this way they finally made their landings.

Within ten minutes of the ramps being lowered, Company "A" had become inert, leaderless, and almost incapable of action. Every officer and sergeant had been killed or wounded . . . . It had become a struggle for survival and rescue. The men in the water pushed wounded men ashore, and those who had reached the sands crawled back into the water pulling others to land to save them from drowning, in many cases only to see the rescued men wounded again or to be hit themselves. Within twenty minutes of striking the beach Company "A" had ceased to be an assault company and had become a forlorn little rescue party bent upon survival and the saving of lives.

Official report, Company "A," 116th Infantry Division

The same reception awaited elements of the 16th IR, 1st Infantry Division, in the eastern sector on Fox Green in front of the Colleville Draw. To the men it was not a question of taking objectives; it was simply a question of self-preservation. There was no let-up from the defensive fire. Anything that moved on the beach became an instant target for the German machine gunners.

Charlie Company of the 2nd Ranger Battalion landed just west of Dog Green sector a few minutes after the ill-fated Able Company of the

A Sherman tank in the Omaha Beach Museum.

116th IR. Their mission was to assault the heights above the Vierville Draw and neutralize any defenses there and, further to the west, at Pointe de la Percée.

The ramps went down on the two LCAs carrying the Rangers and they plunged out into chest-high water. LCA 1038 was raked by machine gun fire and many of the second platoon slumped over in the water, dead or dying. Lieutenant S. Salomon walked off the ramp and immediately lost his footing and floundered under the weight of equipment he was carrying. Sergeant Reed was right behind; as he moved to the left of the ramp he was hit and fell into the water. Lieutenant Salomon looked round and managed to pull the sergeant clear of the surging ramp telling him to make it to the beach the best he could.

Lieutenant Salomon then managed to make it to the base of the cliffs, despite being wounded himself. As the men of LCA 418 started disembarking, the ramp was blown off by a direct hit from a mortar. After receiving another two direct hits the LCA began breaking up. The Rangers had about thirty yards to cover before reaching the base of the cliffs. There they found a crevice in the slope and began to climb using bayonets as hand holds. Once on top the men threw four ropes, secured to stakes, down the cliff face to aid the follow-up troops. Then they immediately started clearing out the defensive positions around a nearby fortified house. Phosphorous grenades were hurled into dugouts and trenches sprayed with machine-gun fire. From their commanding position the Rangers could see the chaos on the beach below. Seeing a boat section from Baker Company of the 116th IR unloading below them, Captain Goranson sent a messenger to show them where the ropes were. These men then reinforced the hard-pressed Rangers. Of the original sixty-five men of the Ranger company, twenty-one had been killed, and eighteen wounded. Only one, Lieutenant William D. Moody, had been killed, shot by a sniper on top of the cliff.

The second wave came in at about 0700 and fared no better. Behind that wave came the 450 men of the 5th Ranger Battalion, accompanied by Able and Baker companies of the 2nd Ranger Battalion. They had been lying offshore awaiting a signal from Pointe du Hoc. If the assault on the coastal gun emplacement at Pointe du Hoc by the 2nd Ranger Battalion was successful, then the second wave was to follow in behind them as reinforcements. If they heard nothing, then they would land on Omaha Beach and take Pointe du Hoc from inland.

Of course, Lieutenant Colonel Max Schneider of the 5th Ranger Battalion was not to know that the assault on Pointe du Hoc was running forty minutes late. He waited an extra fifteen minutes past the allocated time, then headed toward the inferno on the Omaha Beach Sector. Witnessing the chaos before him he decided to land east of their designated landing area in the hope of finding a "quieter spot." It was decided that Dog White was probably the best spot to be as it was still shrouded in smoke, which obscured the enemy's view. They crossed the beach with very few casualties and joined the men of the 116th Infantry Division already sheltering there. Able and Baker Companies were not so lucky. They were to the right of the 5th Ranger Battalion and touched the sector Dog Green. They were cut to pieces. Of about 130 men, only 62 made it to the sea wall. One of the LCAs, carrying these Rangers, was blown to pieces at the water's edge.

These determined Rangers started to probe forward, fighting their way up the bluffs in small groups. Men from the 116th Infantry Division began to join them. Rangers from Able Company were among the first ones to reach the top. This was at about 0830. Looking east they could see their brothers from the 5th Ranger Battalion were also making their way upward. It was actions such as this that finally broke the deadlock and got men moving from the beach.

Wave after wave of men and equipment continued to land on

Omaha Beach, much of it well out of sequence and in disarray, fresh fodder for the German cannons. As each wave landed, more bodies and supplies piled up at the water's edge. To the west, three companies of the 2nd Ranger Battalion, under the command of Lieutenant Colonel James Rudder, were tasked with the assault on the German gun emplacements on Pointe du Hoc, situated on the top of cliffs some thirty-five meters (100 feet) high. On completion of this task they were then expected to form a road block on the blacktop road behind Pointe du Hoc in order to keep German reinforcements from reaching Omaha from the direction of Grandcamp and Maisy. It was hoped that the Rangers would be relieved by the 116th Infantry Division, who had landed on Omaha by noon on D-Day.

Bringing in the three Ranger companies were ten LCAs from the transport ships, both converted ferry steamers, the *Ben My Chree* and the *Amsterdam*. LCA 860 carrying Captain Harold K. Slater and twenty men of Dog Company sank in the choppy seas. The men were later picked up and returned to England, too cold and numb to take any further part in the operation that day.

The remaining nine LCAs plodded on toward the coast. As with other craft, the current had caused the small flotilla to drift eastward. When they realized that it was Pointe de la Percée in front of them, the flotilla immediately altered course, turning west, and began running a course parallel to the coast, back toward Pointe du Hoc. The original plan was for Dog Company to land west of the Pointe du Hoc while Easy and Fox Companies would land on the narrow strip of beach east of the Pointe. Because time had been lost, it was decided on the spur of the moment to land all the craft on the narrow strip to the east. So, the two remaining Dog company LCAs mixed in with the boats carrying Easy and Fox companies. During the Rangers' assault, the battleship *USS Texas* was to bombard the coastline. However, because of the loss of time, the naval bombardment had already stopped when the Rangers went ashore. This gave the German defenders time to recover from the bombardment and to prepare themselves.

Having witnessed the lack of covering fire for the Rangers, the British destroyer, *HMS Talybont,* closed in toward Pointe du Hoc and raked the shore line with gunfire. At the same time the US destroyer, *USS Satterlee,* also came in close and opened up on the enemy positions.

During the aerial and naval bombardments, the small beach area to the east of Pointe du Hoc had been pockmarked with shell holes.

This meant that the four DUKWs (amphibious vehicles), each carrying British fire service extension ladders to be used to scale the cliffs, were ineffective because they could not cross the cratered beach after landing. The men manning the ladders had their machine guns, mounted at the top of the ladders, trained on the German positions, but were unable to hold a steady aim as the ladders swayed from side to side far from the cliffs. To the men watching they resembled a surreal circus act. Back on the LCAs British landing craft personnel helped the beleaguered Rangers as best they could with additional covering fire.

EYEWITNESS

I fired unceasingly with my Lewis Gun at the cliff tops. Germans could be seen running into their positions. I tried to adjust my fire by moving the gun manually and managed to burn my hand badly on the barrel, it was so hot. At the same time a bullet passed by me and broke the broom handle next to me. Silly thing was, I remember thinking at the time of how I was going to explain the broken broom on returning to the mother ship. As we landed bullets were whizzing throughout the craft, but we managed to off-load and reverse away from the beach.
A/B Landing Craft Signalman JF Tolhurst, (author's father) LCA 884

Most of the fire seemed to come down onto the beach from the eastern end of the German defenses. In addition the Germans were rolling hand grenades over the cliff edge and, whenever they had the chance, they also leaned over and fired down onto the Rangers as they climbed up.

Each LCA was fitted with three pairs of rocket-fired grappling hooks. Just before the boats landed, the rockets were fired with the intention of carrying the ropes up and over the high cliffs. The ropes, however, were sodden and heavy and many did not reach the top. The 225 strong Ranger force nevertheless climbed the cliffs with whatever means were at their disposal. Under intense fire and taking many casualties, they eventually managed to reached the top. Amazingly, the first men were up within ten minutes of landing. These highly-trained Rangers proved their courage as they went about their tasks regardless

US 2nd Rangers mark their command post at the cliff edge on Pointe du Hoc with a flag. German prisoners file past in the background.

of the odds stacked against them. If a man found himself alone he would go off individually and get on with the job at hand rather than waiting for others to join him.

As the Rangers fought their way toward the concrete and steel reinforced bunkers, they were shocked to discover that the gun emplacements were in fact empty. The Germans had moved the guns as a result of the weeks of bombing by the Allied air forces prior to the D-Day landings. Lieutenant Colonel James Rudder took his command post from a small cave at the foot of the cliffs to a shell crater on the top of the cliff behind a destroyed German bunker. Using his staff, the walking wounded, and soldiers who had not yet moved inland, he set up a perimeter defense around his headquarters. During this time his

82nd Airborne troops interrogating German prisoners in Orgalandes.

headquarters was taking machine-gun fire from both flanks and snipers seemed to be everywhere. Finally an artillery observer, attached to the Rangers, called down fire from *HMS Talybont*. The ship promptly closed into the shore at Pointe du Hoc and blew the easterly German machine-gun position into the sea. The Rangers then made several attempts to silence the anti-aircraft position now firing at them from the extreme westerly side, but to no avail. Their attack was driven back by intensive fire from both artillery and machine guns. By now Lieutenant Colonel Rudder had himself been wounded twice.

In the meantime, a small force of Rangers had fought their way inland to the road and dug in and begun sending out patrols. One of these patrols consisted of First Sergeant Lommell and Staff Sergeant Kuhn who spotted tracks in the mud leading down a narrow, double hedgerow lane and decided to investigate. There they came across the original Point du Hoc guns, ready to fire, but with no Germans in the immediate vicinity. The two sergeants disabled the guns and returned to their positions.

The Rangers fought off numerous German counter-attacks as their numbers dwindled, but they managed to block and hold the road linking Grandcamp with the Omaha Beach area. By nightfall on June 6th, Colonel Rudder had lost over a third of his force. He had also no word of the situation on Omaha Beach. Although their ammunition was now running low and their rations were nearly non-existent, the men dug in around the orchards south of the highway and continued to beat off constant German counter-attacks. An especially important defense position for the Rangers was that held by Sergeant "Rod" Petty who, armed with his Browning Automatic Rifle (BAR) set up on a nearby wall, was covering a bridge used by the Germans counter-attacking toward the highway. Not many crossed it!

The Rangers' situation was not ideal, but they were under orders to hold their positions until reinforcements from Omaha Beach arrived. Relief was expected that evening, but there was little sign of any help coming. With limited ammunition and supplies, it was now simply a matter of fighting until the reinforcements did arrive or until they ran out of ammunition and the Germans overpowered them.

Back on Omaha, by mid-morning on the 6th, those who were still pinned down on the beach were beginning to realize that staying on the beach was just asking to get killed. So bit by bit the men stirred themselves and began their advance inland.

Lieutenant General Omar Bradley, commander of the 1st US Army Group aboard USS Augusta, was beginning to think that the whole attack on Omaha Beach had been a disaster. Only sketchy messages were coming back from the shore and at one point he contemplated withdrawing his forces from Omaha Beach and sending them, with the rest of the American seaborne forces, directly to Utah Beach where the landing area had almost been secured. When one message arrived, pleading to send more men and not any more vehicles, Bradley obliged and decided to send more infantry into the onslaught in an attempt to break the German defenses.

In the meantime General Cota, assistant divisional commander of the 29th Infantry Division, was darting about the beach totally oblivious to the dangers around him, shouting words of encouragement to the huddled groups of his men. He was heard telling them: "Don't die on the beaches, die up on the bluff if you have to die." Further along the beach other officers were also eager to get their men off the beach and head inland.

EYEWITNESS

"Two kinds of people are staying on this beach. The dead and those who are going to die − now let's get the hell out of here!"
General Taylor, 1st Infantry Division

While Bradley waited for news of any development in the Omaha Sector, the men who were being mercilessly attacked on the beaches began to take heed of the orders and advice they had been given. Small and scattered groups began to get up and advance. Engineers blew gaps in the barbed wire and more and more troops began making their way up the bluffs and away from the open killing ground of the beach area. Eventually Bradley received the much welcomed message he had been waiting for:

EYEWITNESS

Troops formerly pinned down on beaches Easy Red, Easy Green, Fox Red advancing up heights behind beaches.
Message from Gerow's V Corps Headquarters

By the evening the GIs had dragged themselves away from the inferno on the beach and had captured the bluffs. Vierville was in American hands and all five draws leading away from the beach were now secure. Although the Germans still held Colleville and parts of St Laurent, the GIs had them almost surrounded. The cost had been great and V Corps had lost almost 3,000 men. Although they were still well short of their objectives, at least the Allies had now established a firm foothold on Omaha Beach.

By noon the next day, the 29th and 1st Divisions had completed clearing the Omaha Beach area. Though the Germans had counter-attacked Vierville that morning they were held off in the vicinity of the local church and finally driven back. It was during this time that St Laurent and Colleville were also taken and secured.

That same morning a battalion from the 29th Infantry Division aided by the 5th Ranger Battalion and three companies of the 2nd Rangers pushed west along the Grandcamp road. Supported by tanks, their job was to relieve the hard-pressed Ranger force on Pointe du Hoc. The remainder of the 29th remained behind and completed mopping-up operations inland from the beach area. Once this was completed, the 115th Regiment pushed west along the main Bayeux-Isigny highway to capture Longueville.

That afternoon reinforcements from the US 2nd Infantry Division landed on the St Laurent section of Omaha Beach, moved to the top of the bluffs, and went to war. General Gerow's V Corps now consisted of

HMS Glasgow and USS Quincy on station off Cherbourg, June 6th, 1944.

the three infantry divisions the 1st, 2nd, and 29th. By nightfall on the 7th, the three infantry divisions had extended the beachhead out as far as La Cambe and Formigny.

As for the beleaguered Rangers at Pointe du Hoc, they had had to hold out until midday on the 8th when the force from Omaha Beach, after much opposition and numerous skirmishes with the enemy, finally arrived. In the two-and-a-half days of bitter fighting, Lieutenant Colonel Rudder had lost 135 of his 225-man-strong assault force.

Despite the heavy casualties, there was to be no let up in the advance. The attack on the next town and village – Grandcamp and Maisy respectively – started at once. The Germans had failed to destroy the bridge across a small flooded valley. Under constant fire the GIs and Rangers, supported by tanks, made it to the outskirts of Grandcamp. The cruiser *HMS Glasgow* was standing offshore ready

Left and above; a rifle squad moves cautiously through the Bocage. "Digging in" was a regular pastime.

to bombard Grandcamp before the main assault. However, some local fishermen sailed out to the cruiser to tell them it would not be necessary to shell the town. The infantry managed to clear the town of all German resistance by the 9th.

Meanwhile, the 175th IR of the 29th Infantry Division, had made a twelve-mile march and within thirty-six hours was on the outskirts of Isigny. Tanks were sent into the town and found it had been almost completely ruined by the extensive naval bombardment. The tanks met very little resistance as they entered Isigny and the Germans soon retreated without even bothering to demolish the bridge there over the River Aure.

The 1st Infantry Division, meanwhile, had fanned out from the beachhead in a southeasterly direction. By nightfall on the 7th, units of the 16th IR, supported by a force from the 745th Tank Battalion, had smashed straight down the coastal road to Huppain. Only a short distance away was Port-en-Bessin, the dividing line between the British and the American sectors.

V Corps's next operation was to spread further south. Caumont was to be taken by the 1st Infantry Division, Bérigny and Hill 192 by the 2nd, St. Clair-sur-l'Elle and Couvains by the 29th. All these were to be taken by June 12th or 13th. With the exception of Hill 192, all these objectives were accomplished.

At this time V Corps got severely bogged down in the Bocage fighting. XIX Corps had joined them on the left, but it, too, had come to a grinding halt only a few miles from St Lô. Partly this was because the priority in ammunition and equipment was now being assigned to

General Collins' VII Corps for the capture of Cherbourg. V Corps would have to carry on fighting from one hedgerow to another, completely hemmed in, until Cherbourg was safely in American hands; then everything would be focused on the fighting in the south and a way out of the entangled countryside could be sought.

EYEWITNESS

I didn't want to stand up and slug, but . . . at one time we were going to have to. Afterwards we can make the breakthrough and run deep.
Lieutenant General Bradley, commander, 1st US Army Group

V Corps was holding Caumont in the east, but still could not crack Hill 192. In fact, the Germans on Hill 192 would manage to hold out for the rest of June and only after heavy and costly fighting was the hill eventually taken in the beginning of July. The high ground of Clocheville had been defended by crack paratroopers of the German 2nd Corps. During the fighting the US 2nd Infantry Division alone had lost 1,200 men trying to gain the heights.

VIII Corps, on the extreme western flank, was told to take the town of Coutances. Intelligence had advised that opposition would be light. Actually, the 9th and 79th Infantry Divisions sustained horrendous losses and only reached as far as Monte Castre and Mont Gardon, halfway to their objective. The saying went around that, "The Germans haven't much left, but they know how to use it!"

VII Corps reached Sainteny (see Chapter 3), then turned the sector over to VIII Corps and went to join up with the newly arrived XIX Corps north of St Lô. General Corlett's XIX Corps was attacking down the Isigny-St Lô road and was about nine kilometers northeast of St Lô. Now strengthened by the arrival of VII Corps, they renewed their attack on the town.

By July 11th the 35th Infantry Division could see the outskirts of St Lô from a high vantage point. Meanwhile the 29th Infantry Division was approaching the town from the east, in the Martinville area. A week later, the 115th IR began picking its way through the rubble of the eastern side of St Lô. At the same time the 116th IR cautiously started nosing in on the northern side and began their attack. Major Howie of the 3rd Battalion, 116th IR, was killed leading the assault. His men left him by the side of the ruined Sainte Croix Church, covered by the Stars and Stripes.

Finally the German resistance in St Lô dwindled as the Germans withdrew and the town was, at last, in Allied hands. After forty-two successive days of combat, and having sustained many thousands of casualties, it was fitting that the town should fall to the 29th Infantry Division.

The US 1st Army Group had taken four weeks to get where it was, having fought through almost static battles that were reminiscent of World War One. Now suddenly there was room to move. The four corps were soon to be joined by another three, which would constitute General Patton's 3rd Army. The time had come for a change. There must be a breakthrough that would let Patton's 3rd Army charge through and leave behind the infamous Bocage terrain, letting the hemmed-in armored and infantry divisions cut loose. The plan was codenamed Operation Cobra.

EYEWITNESS

It was only step by step, by small groups of five or six men supported by a tank, that we were able to capture one by one the ruins of the last houses and progress along the rubble-clotted streets.
Extract from the 29th Infantry Division Diary

The Americans were to attack on a seven-kilometer-wide front. Opposite them was the German Panzer (Lehr) Division, backed up by the 5th Parachute Division. The start line would be the Périers–St Lô road. Before the attack, the US Army Air Force would drop a carpet of bombs on the German defenses but before the bombing began the attacking divisions of VII Corps pulled back 1,200 meters from the start line as a precaution. Moments later, 2,000 bombers dropped over 4,000 tons of high explosive and napalm into a ten square kilometer area. Only light bombs were dropped because General Bradley did not want deep craters that could impede his armored advance. Unfortunately some of the bombs dropped short, falling among the American troops waiting to go into battle. Among them was Lieutenant General McNair.

Finally on July 25th, seven weeks after D-Day, the attack was launched, from the approximate line we had expected to hold on D plus 5, stretching from Caen through Caumont to St Lô. A tremendous carpet, or area, bombing was placed along the St Lô sector of the American front and its stunning effect upon the enemy lasted throughout the day. Unfortunately a mistake by part of the bombing forces caused a considerable number of casualties in one battalion of the 9th Division and in the 30th Division, and killed General McNair, who had gone into an observation post to watch the beginning of the attack. His death cast a gloom over all who had known this most able and devoted officer.
General Dwight D. Eisenhower, supreme commander of the Allied Expeditionary Force

At 1100 on July 25th, VII Corps launched their attack. Even after all the punishment the Germans had received, they were still able to resist. Tanks from the Panzer (Lehr) Regiment were blown upside down or lay in the bottom of huge bomb craters. Nevertheless, the Germans were masters at salvaging their equipment and managed to repair many of the less-damaged tanks and get them running again. The effect of the bombing on the German infantry, however, resulted in many being killed, wounded, or buried alive; others were too shell-shocked from the deafening and terrifying explosions to fight. Despite this, when VII Corps attacked they found that the Germans still held their positions as stubbornly as ever. Some of the initial attacks by the American infantry were stopped cold and the GIs were forced back.

American infantry in front of our trenches are abandoning their positions. They are withdrawing everywhere.
Report from 440S Panzer Grenadiers to divisional headquarters

There was, however, one weakness in the German defenses. The Germans were fighting in well-defended pockets of resistance, but there was no constant line of defense, so the pockets could be outflanked. This convinced General Collins that his armored divisions could now be let loose.

The US 1st Infantry and elements of the 3rd Armored Division pushed on and bypassed the main German defense pockets. This allowed them to reach Marigny. The 2nd Armored Division carried on into Canisy and by the end of the 26th both places had been secured. The following day the 1st Infantry and 3rd Armored Divisions struck southwest and gained another five miles by taking Cerisy-la-Salle.

VIII Corps was continuing to make its way south from Périers and Lessay, well on its way to Coutances. Generalleutnant Dietrich von Choltitz, commander of the German 84th Corps in the region, realized that he was about to be cut off by the Americans as they advanced south. So he began to withdraw his forces to escape the oncoming rush of US divisions. By the time the 1st Infantry and 3rd Armored Division cut the Coutances-Granville road on July 29th the majority of the Germans had

St Lô after its capture.

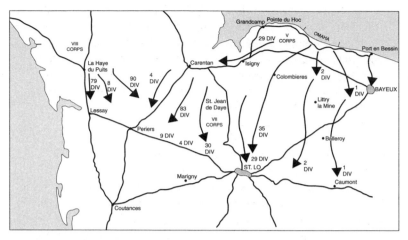

Tiger tanks rumble forward to reinforce German positions.

managed to escape. When the 4th Armored Division finally liberated Coutances on July 30th they found that the Germans had already gone. Behind them, though, the Germans had littered Coutances with booby traps.

Three of the German divisions, retreating to the southeast, were caught in the open, around the village of Roncey, by American fighter bombers that strafed them and destroyed many of their vehicles. The 2nd Armored Division managed to trap nearly 3,000 enemy troops of the 2nd and 17th SS Divisions while another 1,500 Germans were captured in an ambush at St Denis-le-Gast.

The break-out from the Bocage countryside was gaining momentum. At last the Americans were shaking free of the troublesome Germans and the difficult terrain. On August 1st the newly arrived 3rd Army under General Patton stormed through the Allied lines. Patton immediately sent the 4th and 6th Armored Divisions from Coutances crashing through to Avranches. Patton's theory was to give the enemy no time to reorganize and instead keep him under severe pressure at all times. Regardless of the lack of protection offered to his flanks by the slow-moving infantry of the VII Corps, he decided to race on.

To the east, V and XIX Corps were still being held up in the Bocage country around Tessy and Torigny-sur-Vire. The men of the 29th, 30th, and 35th Infantry Divisions had to fight a four-day battle from July 27th to the 31st, in order to break through the German positions. Between them the two corps amassed over 1,800 casualties. Tessy fell on August 1st and XIX Corps could at last push on toward Vire. On the same day, tanks of the 4th Armored Division found the bridge over the River Sélune at Pontaubault still intact. It was a lucky find. The route into Bretagne [Brittany] was now clear and the tank commanders made full use of it.

The overall plan was for VIII Corps to drive on toward Brent. The three corps of the 3rd Army were on their way to the River Loire, to the River Seine, and to the town of Orleans. It was hoped that this penetration would drive the Germans out of Brittany and enable the Allies to capture more deep water ports to service the ever-increasing demands for supplies and troops. It was also hoped that this would enable the Allies to encircle all the German forces that were fighting in Normandy between the rivers Seine and Loire.

On August 3rd, the 1st Infantry Division entered Mofirtain. It was here that the Germans decided to counterattack in force attempting to drive on to the coast and split the two American armies in half. On August 7th the Germans attacked from their front line between Sourdeval and Barenton. The US 30th Infantry Division was driven out of Mortain and the town was recaptured by the Germans. The following day the Americans regrouped and recovered from the surprise attack. With the aid of the US air force, the attacking Germans were stopped. During the next four days the fighting was intense, but by the 12th the Germans started to give way and slowly withdraw. The last full scale attack to hit the Americans, west of the River Seine, had been thwarted.

With Patton's 3rd Army sweeping around south and east, and the British and Canadian troops pressing toward Falaise, the Germans were being pushed into a pocket around Mortain, Argentan, and Falaise. General Patton wanted to drive north and close the gap, thus sealing the fate of the German armies west of the Seine immediately. His superiors, however, were more cautious and would not allow such a brash move. Patton was ordered to drive east to the River Seine and form a block there. XV Corps was given the task of forming the southern jaw of the trap. The Falaise gap was closing and the end of the Battle of Normandy was at last in sight (see Chapter 7).

CIRCUIT FOUR

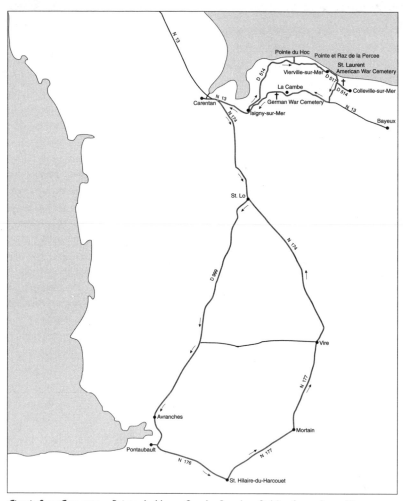

Circuit four. Carentan – Pointe du Hoc – Omaha Beach – St Lô – Avranches – Vire

S TARTING FROM CARENTAN TAKE THE INFAMOUS old N-13 east to Isigny. (Note that there is now a new N-13 autoroute that bypasses Carentan and Isigny). Here the town was destroyed by Allied bombing and artillery. The 29th Infantry liberated the town during the night of June 8th/9th. In the center of town in the Place de Gaulle is a monument recalling the D-Day landings. The monument also honors the speech addressed to the liberated French by General de Gaulle in Bayeux on June 4th, 1944. Continue through Isigny-sur-Mer and through the next village of Osmanville to join the D-514 signposted Grandcamp-Maisy. This town has a close tie to the US Rangers, and the veteran Rangers always stay here when visiting the area for anniversaries or vacations. The Hotel du Guesclin is a recommended stay. The prices are very reasonable, with friendly staff, good food, and a sea view. (Whenever my father – one of the crewman on LCA 884 – and I have stayed there for the anniversaries we have been treated royally.) About fifty yards from the hotel is the Rangers Museum on the sea front.

This is a small but quite interesting museum dedicated to the Rangers at Pointe du Hoc. Contained inside are many artifacts donated by veterans from the Rangers, as well as a thorough but concise rundown on how the Pointe du Hoc operations were carried out. There is also a film, with some excellent footage of the invasion.

Carry on through the town back onto the D-514, and continue until you see the signpost, and a left turn, for Pointe du Hoc. A short drive down this road will bring you to an ample parking lot. This thirty-acre battlefield has been preserved as it was left back in 1944, the only addition being the fencing and footpaths for the visitor's safety. A walk around here will allow you to explore the German troop shelters and bunkers. At the northernmost point a needle-like memorial to the 2nd Ranger Battalion stands atop an observation bunker. Below, in the bunker itself, is a memorial plaque that lists all the Rangers who lost their lives in the fighting to take this area. Still visible on the concrete bunkers and shelters are the blast marks of grenades and the bullet scars that indicate the ferociousness of the fighting here.

From Pointe du Hoc take the D-514 east to Vierville-sur-Mer. On the left is the new Omaha Beach Museum (opened in time for the 55th anniversary of the landings in 1999). Just past the museum, to the right hand of the road, is a large château. On the entrance gate post is a memorial plaque in recognition that this building was used as the headquarters of the US Army Eleventh Port from June 8th to July 2nd 1944.

Take the left turn, almost opposite the château, down onto Omaha Beach. This was exit D-1 from the beach, the Vierville Draw. Look out for several memorials, on either side of the road, as you make your way down to the sea front. On the left, a plaque to the Rangers, to your right memorials to the 29th Infantry Division and US 6th Engineer Special Brigade. Take a right turn along the beach road. On the corner, to the left, is a German bunker and a large monument dedicated to the US National Guard, (of which the 29th Infantry Division was part).

Also to the left, on the sands, is a small jetty. This is built on all that now remains of the American "Mulberry Harbor" that was built but later destroyed during the great storm of June 19th, 1944 (better examples of part of the Mulberry Harbor can be seen off the coast of Arromanches – (see Chapter 6).

The area in front of you is Dog Green beach. To the left, immediately in front of the high cliffs, is Charlie beach. This is the area where the hapless Able Company of the 116th IR and Charlie Company of the 2nd Ranger Battalion hit the beaches on D-Day. Just a look around, even today with most of the positions covered, will tell you that this must have been hell for the men trying to cross the open beach at mid-tide. Alongside the beach road there is now a café and gift shop, which are worth a visit and not particularly expensive.

Travel along the beach road and you will be passing through the different sectors of Omaha Beach. Midway on the right is a small monument marking the site of the first American cemetery in France after D-Day. Bodies from here were later moved to the American Military Cemetery and Memorial between St Laurent-sur-Mer and Colleville-sur-Mer.

Further along the beach, on the left, is a small inconspicuous plaque that commemorates the landing of one of many raids that were carried out by British Commandos prior to the D-Day landings. In this raid, on September 12th, 1942, Major Gus March-Phillips and three of his men were killed in a firefight on Omaha Beach. Today three of them rest in the churchyard in St Laurent-sur-Mer.

Follow the beach road around to the right and past the large Comité du Débarquement monument on the left hand side. From the roundabout/rotary, take the road that leads up toward St Laurent-sur-Mer. This is the second beach exit D-3, the Les Moulins Draw. This was also the dividing line between the 29th Infantry Division and the 1st

Infantry Division and marks the line where Easy Green changes to the Easy Red sector. Just up from here on the right stands the Omaha Beach Museum. Outside is a 155mm Long Tom and a Sherman tank. Visiting this museum is thoroughly recommended: the collection of equipment and gear inside is superb.

Return to the beach road and head east where, on the right, is a superb restaurant called Le Ruquet. When digging the foundations for this restaurant they found the remains of an LCVP. Further along, the road narrows to a lane and leads to a small parking lot. Around this area are more fortifications and memorials. Continue inland along the lane and up the third beach exit E-1, the St Laurent Draw. Carry on through St Laurent-sur-Mer until you reach the D-514. Now take a left turn and follow the signs for the American Military Cemetery and Memorial until you take a left turn into its grounds.

After parking in the large parking lot, make your way on foot to the cemetery. At the entrance to the cemetery is a small visitors' center that contains offices and a comfortable lounge for anyone who wishes to visit. The staff here is very knowledgeable and helpful and will always try to help anyone who has questions about the cemetery or wishes to know the location of a particular headstone.

The whole area has been given to the US in perpetuity and the grounds are magnificent, with well-manicured lawns and beautifully kept gardens. It slopes gently toward the sea and the white marble headstones of the 9,386 American soldiers buried here are lined up on a well-tended lawn. It is a very moving sight. Of the 9,386 headstones here, 307 mark the graves of "Unknowns." In addition, a further 14,000 servicemen, killed in the Battle for Normandy, were returned home at the request of their next of kin. Also buried here, side by side, are a father and his son, and in thirty-three instances two brothers also rest side by side. Most of the dead buried here gave their lives in the landing operations and in the establishment of the beachhead. The headstones are of white Italian marble, and represent all religious denominations. Near the center of the cemetery is a round chapel with an overhanging roof supported by square pillars. Inside a beautiful mosaic ceiling depicts the sacrifices of the American troops.

At the eastern end of the cemetery is a memorial fronted by a large rectangular pool. The memorial (the work of architects Harbeson, Hough, Livingston, and Larson) is composed of two pavilions linked by a crescent-shaped portico circling a terrace. In the center of the portico, a nude allegorical figure raises both arms to the sky, "The Spirit of American Youth," sculpted by Donald de Lue. On the front of the portico, the inscription reads: "This shore, marked by battle, portal of Liberty, is forever sanctified by the ideals, the courage and the sacrifice of our companions." On the interior walls of the two pavilions, is a map of the military operations. On the facade of the pavilion on the right, the inscription translated from the French reads: "The United States of America, proud of the achievements of its sons, humble in front of their sacrifice, have erected this monument to honor their memory."

Behind the memorial, down a short flight of steps, there is a garden and low wall on which are inscribed the names of 1,557 soldiers who have no known grave.

Follow the path from the memorial to the sea and there you will find an observation platform that overlooks the Easy Red sector of Omaha beach and the fourth beach exit, E3 – the Colleville Draw.

Return to your car and drive back to the roundabout/rotary on the D-514, at the main entrance. Take the left hand road to Colleville-sur-Mer. Just after the church, in Colleville-sur-Mer, take a left turn down a small lane (the fifth exit, F-1) to the beach and park in the parking lot there. There is much to do and see in the Omaha beach area and it is probably best to leave the car parked and hike around to see all the sights. There are many installations and fortifications up on the bluffs, so, provided you are not walking on private property, it is worth a look around.

When you return to your car drive back up the narrow lane and follow the one-way system back into the US Cemetery grounds. Return to the roundabout/rotary on the D-514 but this time take a right turn along the D-514 and return to St Laurent-sur-Mer.

At the crossroads at St Laurent-sur-Mer take a left turn onto the D-517 signposted Formigny. This village had an important crossroads and had been protected by three batteries of 150mm field guns in positions at the hamlet of Montigny. The village was finally liberated on June 8th.

Now join the N-13 in the direction of Cherbourg and head for La Cambe. Take the turning for La Cambe and follow the signs for the German cemetery. This cemetery is the largest of all the war cemeteries in Normandy, with over 21,000 German soldiers buried in the grounds. Among them is the grave of SS Hauptsturmführer Michel Wittmann (see Chapter 6). In the center of the cemetery is a grassed mound under which rest 296 bodies in a mass grave. Just outside the entrance of La

Cambe cemetery is an exhibition and peace garden.

Return to the N-13 and continue in the direction of Cherbourg. Exit at the junction signposted Carentan and St Lô and take the N-174 toward St Lô. One kilometer south of the town of St Jean-de-Daye is a roundabout/rotary. Take a right turn onto the D-8 and go to le Dézert. There, in the village, is a 50mm anti-tank gun on display. This village was totally destroyed and only rebuilt between 1950 and 1960. Return to the N-174 and turn right for St Lô.

In the center of St Lô is La Place du Major Howie. There is also a bust beside the church of Sainte Croix. In the center of a roundabout/rotary on the road that leads to Bayeux is a monument to the sacrifice of 8,000 GIs. Outside the town hall in the Place de l'Hotel de Ville a memorial has been erected to the French resistance. It is made from the door of the old prison where forty-two resistance fighters died. Locked in their cells, they were killed by an Allied air raid. Many of the outlying villages were also destroyed during the fighting, and all have their own tale to tell.

Proceed through St Lô and out onto the D-999 Voie de la Liberté (Liberty Highway) leading to Avranches. In Avranches is a memorial commemorating General Patton and his 3rd Army.

Out of Avranches head south to Pontaubault. Here, the gateway to Brittany, over 1,000 vehicles crossed the bridge during August 1944. A short way further south is the American cemetery at St James which contains 4,410 graves.

After Pontaubault, turn left, heading for St Hilaire-du-Harcouët. In the center of town, at the crossroads, turn left for Mortain. Here, of course, was the scene of the great German counterattack on the night of August 6th. Around this town was some of the heaviest fighting in the entire campaign. It was not recaptured until August 12th after heavy fighting and terrible losses on both sides.

From here proceed north on the N-177 to Vire. This town was liberated on August 8th. Pass through Vire on the N-174 back toward St Lô. This will take you through Tessy/Torigny-sur-Vire, scene of the great debacle of the 29th, 30th, and 35th Infantry Divisions who faced the German 2nd Parachute Corps here between July 27th and 31st. The US divisions lost about 1,800 men here in the four days of conflict. Tessy was finally captured in the evening of August 1st. With this task completed, XIX Corps was allowed to push on toward Vire.

From here remain on the N-174, which will take you back to St Lô.

5
SWORD BEACH TO CAEN

THE LANDINGS ON SWORD BEACH started well, despite the swell caused by the recent storms, which meant that the tide was higher than expected. The LCOCU boys (Landing Craft Obstacle Clearance Units) had done a good job during the previous forty-eight hours, approaching the landing beaches in their midget submarines and clearing away some of the underwater obstacles. They had also marked the landing area well, insuring that the first waves came ashore at the right place.

The British 3rd Infantry Division, comprised of the 8th, 185th, and 9th Infantry Brigades, with No. 1 Special Service Brigade in support, made up the assault force for Sword Beach. Following a naval bombardment that began at 0650, the first troops of the 8th Infantry Brigade made the initial landings at La Brèche (now called La Brèche d'Hermanville) at 0725. The brigade was comprised of one battalion each from the South Lancashires, the East Yorks, and the Suffolks. Preceding the infantry were the DD tanks of the 13th/18th Hussars, which landed to provide covering fire for the AVRE tanks of the 5th Assault Regiment, Royal Engineers, who immediately began clearing the beach obstacles and beach exits for the infantry. Many of the engineers were killed as they disembarked from their landing craft. Among them was their commanding officer Lieutenant Colonel A. Cocks, who was killed when his landing craft received two direct hits just after unloading a Crab flail tank. The second explosion detonated a supply of Bangalore torpedoes, which killed the officer and other engineers.

Despite this, each man had his job to do and selflessly continued with his work. Minutes later the infantry stormed the beaches, with the two assault companies of the South Lancashires landing to the west. The right hand company was tasked with clearing the beach of the German defenses and exploiting their position along the beach to the west. The left hand company meanwhile would clear its own area of beach, then launch an attack against the German strongpoint at La Brèche, codenamed Cod. The right hand company of the East Yorks would also help destroy the strongpoint while the left hand company made its way toward Riva Bella and Ouistreham. The Suffolks would land within the hour and reinforce the troops at La Brèche before moving inland toward the village of Colleville (now called Colleville-Montgomery). Once the village was liberated they would then attack the German fortifications known as "Hillman."

EYEWITNESS

The boat crews had been ordered to go in at 4 knots and hit the beach hard. During the last hundred yards of the run-in everything seemed to happen at once. Out of the haze of smoke underwater obstacles loomed up . . . . We weaved in between iron rails and ramps and pickets with tella-mines on top like gigantic mushrooms. We seemed to be groping through a grotesque petrified forest. The noise was so continuous that it seemed like a siren . . . . Mortar fire was coming down on the sands, an 88mm gun was firing along the line of the beach and there was continuous machine-gun and rifle fire. Immediately ahead of us a DD tank, its rear end enveloped in flames, unable to get off the beach, continued to fire its guns.

Major A. Rouse, 1st Battalion, the South Lancashire Regiment

Also landing at La Brèche, just before the Suffolks, were the commandos of Brigadier The Lord Lovat's No. 1 Special Service Brigade. This unit was made up of Nos. 3, 4, and 6 Commando, No. 45 (Royal Marine) Commando, and elements of the Free-French commandos of 1 and 8 troop of No. 10 (Inter-Allied) Commando. No. 4 Commando was ordered to destroy any beach defenses that had not yet been silenced by the infantry or by the pre-assault naval and aerial bombardments. After that, with the French commandos leading the way, they would storm the German Battery known as "the Casino" at Riva Bella in Ouistreham. In the meantime, the rest of Lord Lovat's commandos would follow, ready to make their way across the six-and-a-half miles of enemy held territory to form the link–up between the airborne and seaborne troops at Bénouville (Pegasus) Bridge.

To the west, Brigadier B. "Jumbo" Leicester's No. 4 Special Service (Royal Marine) Brigade would land on the right flank of the Sword invasion force near Lion-sur-Mer. Part of his force, No. 47 Commando landed separately from the Brigade, at Le Hamel (Gold Beach), since its objective was the coastal port of Port-en-Bessin (see Chapter 6). The rest of the commandos, however, were ordered to take the coastal villages of Lion-sur-Mer, Luc-sur-mer, and Langrune-sur-Mer.

No. 48 (Royal Marine) Commando, landing at St Aubin-sur-Mer (Juno Beach), captured a strongpoint at Langrune-sur-Mer (Juno Beach) while No. 46 (Royal Marine) Commando, under the cover of a naval bombardment, captured a strongpoint at Le Petit Enfer in Luc-sur-Mer. They then sent two troops inland to take the village of La Délivrande. Later these units would move further inland and take the villages of Rots and Le Hamel near the main Bayeux to Caen Highway.

No. 41 (Royal Marine) Commando, meanwhile, landed at Lion-sur-Mer and captured the village before moving on to its next objective, the radar station at Douvres. This heavily fortified strongpoint managed to hold out for eleven days before being captured. Since it was on the demarcation line between the Canadian and British sector both British and Canadian divisions contributed to the capture of the radar station.

Back at La Brèche, leading the No. 1 Special Service Brigade landings, was No. 4 Commando led by Lieutenant Colonel Robert Dawson. Also under his command was Commandant Philippe Kieffer and the two French Commando troops. As the landing craft surged through the white surf, line abreast, in defiance of the German mortar and shell fire, Lieutenant Colonel Dawson ordered his landing craft skipper to slow down so that the two landing craft carrying the French Commandos could claim the honor of being the first commandos to step onto the French beaches on D-Day.

As the commandos ran through the breakwaters they found that many of the infantrymen were still pinned down at the water's edge, crouching or lying in two of three feet of water, taking cover from the murderous German machine-gun fire and incessant explosions of mortar rounds. Passing through the infantry, the commandos stormed a German strongpoint responsible for much of the fire. Cutting their way through the barbed wire defenses they crossed a minefield and paused long enough for the rest of the commandos to assemble. Within the first few minutes of battle the commandos had lost over forty men on the beach. Among them, Lieutenant Colonel Dawson was twice wounded, first in the leg, which he ignored, and then, more seriously, a head wound that forced him to relinquish command to his second in command, Major R. Menday.

Behind them Lord Lovat landed with the rest of No. 1 Special Service Brigade. Among them was Lovat's piper Bill Millin (later to be known as the "Mad Piper of Normandy") holding his bagpipes aloft as he waded ashore;

Memorial to Commandant Phillipe Kieffer, next to the French Commando memorial.

French Commando Memorial at Ouistreham. (See also page 133.)

EYEWITNESS

Once I could find my feet, I started to play "The Highland Laddie," the regimental quick march of the Scots Guards, as I went ashore. The Brigadier had been involved with military training with the regiment, and it brought a smile to his face . . . . At one stage, a large figure looked me up and down, then bellowed in my ear in an angry voice: "You mad bastard. . . ." It was a commando sergeant.
Piper Bill Millin, No. 1 Special Service Brigade

The leading commandos paused only long enough to allow their men to reassemble, then the French Commandos led the way along the road, which runs parallel to the beach, toward the German coastal battery at Riva Bella. With the help of a local gendarme who was a member of the French resistance, they were able to circle many of the German strongpoints and take up position for their assault on the battery. But despite a heavy naval bombardment to soften up the defenses, the solid walls of the concrete fortification were only partially damaged. The defenders inside were very much alive. The French Commandos only managed to overpower the shell-shocked Germans after a violent and vicious hand-to-hand battle that cost both sides many casualties. As soon as the battle was over the exhausted fighting troops witnessed one of the many, almost surreal, emotive scenes that face men in times of war: the sight of French, British, and German medical orderlies working together to tend the dead and dying who littered the battlefield.

By mid-morning the South Lancashires had liberated Hermanville, the Suffolks had taken Colleville, and the East Yorks and No. 1 Special Service Brigade were holding Ouistreham. With Ouistreham liberated, Lord Lovat was able to press on toward the bridges over the Caen Canal and River Dives to help reinforce the 6th Airborne Division. One obstacle, however, still represented a danger to any troops moving south from Ouistreham. This was Hillman, the German strongpoint mentioned earlier. Situated southeast of Colleville, together with a satellite strongpoint, Morris, to the north, the two German positions commanded a field of fire that stretched north to the landing beaches and east across St Aubin-d'Arquenay toward the Caen Canal.

The Suffolks pushed on past Colleville and managed to take

British 17-pounder anti-tank gun crew.

strongpoint Morris by 1300. Hillman, however, was a much tougher target.

As the Suffolks prepared their attack on Hillman, 185th Brigade landed at La Brèche and began moving toward their objective – the high ground north of Caen from Beuville, Biéville, and Lébisey. If successful, they would attempt to take Caen itself. At the same time, the 9th Brigade would attempt to take Mathieu, Cambes-en-Plaine, and up

EYEWITNESS

The area covered was approximately 600 yards by 400 yards containing three steel cupolas, deep concrete shelters, infantry guns, machine guns, etc., very well dug in and camouflaged; it was the local Coastal Battalion HQ*, surrounded by wire, anti-tank mines and anti–personnel mines.
Captain Sperling, Regimental Signals Officer, 1st Battalion, the Suffolk Regiment

* *[In fact it was the Regimental HQ of the 736th Grenadier Regiment.]*

to St Contest, the area that lay between the 185th Brigade and the 3rd Canadian Infantry Division.

The 1st Battalion, The Royal Norfolk Regiment, were given orders to bypass Hillman in order to reach their objective. Believing the village of St Aubin-sur-Mer to be still in enemy hands (in fact Lord Lovat's No 1 Special Service Brigade had already cleared the village) the battalion set off from Colleville, across the wheat fields between the village and the German strongpoint, to Beuville. The German sentries at Hillman spotted the advance and opened up with their machine guns at a range of half a mile. Within minutes the Norfolks had lost 150 men. The cries from the

Panzer tank and crew of the 12th SS (Hitler Jugend) Panzer Division, await orders on June 6th, 1944.

wounded were still echoing around the battlefield as the Suffolks launched their attack on the fortress. Sappers managed to breach the barbed wire perimeters with Bangalore torpedoes. PIATS (anti-tank weapons) were fired at the steel cupolas to no effect. The Norfolks managed to capture some of the outer trenches and take a few prisoners, but they were unable to penetrate the solid German defenses.

124

In a second attack, the tanks of the 13th/18th Hussars were brought in, but even their seventeen-pounder armor-piercing shells were unable to penetrate the steel cupolas. But with the cover provided by the tanks, the infantry were eventually able to overpower the German defenders and Hillman was cleared of enemy resistance at just after 2000.

The German units defending Sword Beach were from the 736th Grenadier Regiment of the 716th Coastal Defense Division. By mid-afternoon, however, reinforcements were on their way from Generalleutnant Feuchtinger's 21st Panzer Division. Deployed around St. Pierre-sur-Dives, the 21st Panzer Division had been the closest armored division to the area of the invasion. Some of its units were actually on anti-invasion exercise during the night of June 5th/6th and were therefore immediately drawn into action, east of Caen, in an attempt to repulse the landings of the 6th Airborne Division.

Due to a complicated chain of command and commitments against the British airborne forces, Feuchtinger's panzer tanks did not arrive in the Sword area until late afternoon. This was reported by a reconnaissance troop of the Staffordshire Yeomanry who had, along with the 1st Battalion, The King's Own Scottish Borderers, passed through Hermanville and secured Beuville and Biéville. As the leading elements of the British 3rd Infantry Division neared their objective of Caen, Feuchtinger's 21st Panzer Division was already preparing to launch its counterattack. Hastily digging in and holding the line from Lébisey to la Londe, the Germans held the high ground that dominated the approach to Caen. With less than three miles to go, the British advance was stopped in its tracks. Also approaching, on the German left flank, were the fanatical troops of the 12th SS (Hitler Jugend) Panzer Division, commanded by Oberstgruppenführer Witt.

On the evening of D-Day a gap remained between the British and Canadian bridgeheads, between Lion-sur-Mer and Luc-sur-Mer. In the early evening, the 21st Panzer Division set off to exploit this gap, pushing down from Caen toward Biéville and Mathieu, in the hope of reaching the coast and pushing the Allies back into the sea. Luckily, the British were prepared for such an attack and, with well-sited seventeen-pounder anti-tank guns on the high ground at Périers, they managed to stop the main German advance. Only one company of German infantry and a handful of tanks managed to get through and make their way toward the beach. The advance, however, coincided with the arrival of the largest airlift in military history. And there is little doubt that this sight took the heart out of the German's resolve to put in a sustained and coordinated attack.

At 2100, less than an hour after the German strongpoint of Hillman had been captured, a massive air armada of gliders and planes brought in much-needed supplies at the two drop and landing zones on either side of the Caen Canal. German troops in the vicinity opened fire with everything they had, filling the sky with a peppering of flak and streaks of tracer fire. Protecting the 500-plus supply-carrying aircraft were fighter escorts of Spitfires and Mustangs. They swooped down and attacked the German ground positions while the gliders landed in fields that were being bombarded by German artillery and mortar fire. The much-needed supplies had arrived and so, too, had the reinforcements needed to hold the fragile airborne bridgehead east of the River Orne.

By the end of the first day, despite Caen not having fallen, and without a link-up to the Canadian troops from Juno Beach, the Sword beach landings were considered a success. The seaborne troops had managed to linkup and reinforce the 6th Airborne Division and, more importantly, they had also drawn Rommel's panzer reserves in and around Caen. This took the pressures, at least temporarily, off the 50th Northumbrian Division landing on Sword Beach, and the American troops to the west at Omaha and on the Cherbourg Peninsular. For those American soldiers still fighting to gain a foothold on the shores of Omaha Beach, it would prove to be an especially important respite.

By June 10th, the British 3rd Infantry Division held a line that ran from Blainville-sur-Orne, on the banks of the Caen Canal, up to the Canadian boundary line just west of Cambes–en-Plaine. It became a static battle, reminiscent of World War One, with neither side willing to relinquish any ground and with a no-man's land, stretching for less than 100 yards in some places, between the two armies. With the failure to take and hold Villers-Bocage and envelop Caen in Operation Perch (see Chapter 6), General Montgomery and Lieutenant General Miles Dempsey, commander of the British Second Army, decided to launch an attack across the Rivers Odon and Orne to the southwest of Caen. Codenamed Operation Epsom, the main attack would be made by the British VIII Corps in an attempt to reach the high ground between Bretteville-sur-Laize and Bourguébus. With this accomplished the 3rd Canadian and 3rd British Infantry Divisions could then close in on Caen and isolate the German forces in the city. Twenty-four hours before the main assault, XXX Corps launched their attack first, toward

A Bren gun carrier and "flail" tank of the 15th Scottish Division ready for Operation Epsom.

the high ground southeast of Tilly-sur-Seulles, to protect VIII Corps' right flank.

The 15th Scottish Division and 11th Armored Division led the attack for VIII Corps just before dawn on June 26th, making their way slowly through the villages of St Manvieu, Cheux, and a nearby hamlet. By the end of the day they had progressed four miles from their start line but were still one mile from the River Odon. The enemy troops in this area, from the 12th SS Panzer Division, fought with great tenacity and determination. Eventually the tanks of the 11th Armored Division made it across the River Odon and were fighting on the slopes of Hill 112. The Germans threw everything they had against the British and the battle raged around the hill.

Two days later, General Dollmann, commander of the German Seventh Army, ordered that Oberstgruppenführer Paul Hausser's 2nd Panzer Corps should immediately attack the British VIII Corps with his 9th and 10th Panzer Divisions. This attack, toward the villages of Gavrus and Cheux, failed when the British troops defending the villages refused to move or retreat despite heavy losses.

On the morning of June 29th, the 11th Armored Division had taken possession of Hill 112. This gave the British a commanding view of the German positions. Accurate and sustained shellfire throughout the day and following night kept any German counter-offensive in check. Aerial reconnaissance photographs and reports revealed, however, a continued build–up of German armor. Lieutenant General Dempsey was fearful of overstretching his communication and supply lines and believed that his men were exhausted and too exposed to fight off another attack from Hausser's fresh Panzer Divisions. He therefore decided to order the advance to stop, and he withdrew the 11th Armored Division back over the River Odon. The following day Hill 112 was re-taken by the Germans. Operation Epsom had failed in its main objective, and had cost VIII Corps over 4,000 casualties, but it had not all been in vain. The German panzer divisions had received a severe mauling and General Dollmann had panicked about the growing Allied bridgehead. Fearing Hitler's reprisals, he committed suicide on the morning of June 29th. On the same day Generalfeldmarschall von Rundstedt and Generalfeldmarschall Rommel were visiting Hitler at Berchtesgaden, thus leaving the German troops in Normandy without their three most senior commanders. Hausser, who would soon succeed Dollmann in command of the Seventh Army (becoming the first SS officer to command a German field army), followed Dollmann's last orders, despite not having

Sherman tanks of the 11th Armored Division on June 25th in Operation Epsom.

his panzer divisions at full strength. The swift rebuttal of his panzers by the British led Hausser to concede that it was time for the German forces to withdraw from Caen, and he relayed his report to Rommel's HQ to that effect:

EYEWITNESS

The counter-offensive by the 1st and 2nd Panzer Corps has had to be temporarily suspended in the face of intensive enemy artillery fire and supporting fire unprecedented ferocity from naval units... the tenacious enemy resistance will prevent our counter-offensive from having any appreciable effect . . . [we should] husband the resources of the panzer divisions and create a defensive line commensurate with our infantry strength.

Oberstgruppenführer Paul Hausser, 2nd SS Panzer Corps

Von Rundstedt and Rommel shared Hausser's view and suggested to Hitler that the Seventh Army should begin to fight a rearguard action back toward the River Seine. Hitler would hear nothing of it. He ordered that the Allied bridgehead must be contained and the Allies forced into a war of attrition; meanwhile, the Germans would build up their own supplies and force the Allies back into the sea. Hitler's plans, however, could not match his resources and von Rundstedt knew this. In a telephone call on July 1st from Generalfeldmarschall von Kluge, von Rundstedt was asked what should be done now that they faced an ever increasing Allied force. Von Rundstedt had resigned himself to the futility of his command and made his reply direct and succinct, "Make peace, you fools. What else can you do?"

Von Rundstedt's comments were passed on to Hitler who immediately relieved him of his position. Generalfeldmarschall von Kluge was named his successor.

The fighting around Hill 112 continued for over a month and included another offensive, Operation Jupiter, which was launched by the 43rd Wessex Division on July 10th. This, too, failed after a strong counterattack by SS panzer tanks. In the meantime, the Canadians had launched Operation Charnwood (see Chapter 7) in an attempt to dislodge the German defenders in Caen itself.

The next major offensive for the British armored divisions was Operation Goodwood, which was launched in conjunction with the Canadian Offensive of Operation Atlantic (see Chapter 7). It began on the morning of July 18th after a 1,000 bomber raid in which over 5,000 tons of fragmentation bombs were dropped on the German defenses. 700 tanks of VIII Corps then rolled forward, heading south, through the 6th Airborne Division's area of operations east of the River Orne. It was hoped that the British armored advance would destroy all the German equipment and personnel on its way to the high ground around Bourguébus. Once this had been taken they could then push on and sweep across the open plains, south of Caen, toward Falaise. In the meantime the Canadians would attack the center of Caen and clear the city of German resistance.

EYEWITNESS

I knew all along that the German position in France was hopeless and that eventually the war would be lost. But if I had been given a free hand to conduct operations, I think I could have made the Allies pay a fearful price for their victory. I had planned to fight a slow retiring action exacting a heavy toll for each bit of ground that I gave up. I hoped that this might have brought about a political decision which would have saved Germany from complete and utter defeat. But I did not have my way. As commander in chief in the west my only authority was to change the guard in front of my gate.

Generalfeldmarschall von Rundstedt, Commander in Chief, West

Rommel, though, had anticipated such an attack and had prepared five lines of defenses that were up to ten miles deep between the British front line and their objective. With a fire power in excess of 1,500 guns, the Germans dug in and waited for the British armor to roll into its killing ground. Subsequently the German lines were not broken and the British attack was stopped after an advance of only seven miles. After two days' bitter and costly fighting, the British had lost nearly 400 tanks and had sustained over 5,500 casualties. The Canadians, though, had managed to clear the southern suburbs of Caen and so Montgomery prepared another offensive, led by the Canadians, to secure the objectives originally planned for Goodwood. This was codenamed Operation Spring, and began in the early hours of July 25th (see Chapter 7).

By now the Germans were unable to resupply their front line as quickly as the British. They had also lost another of their commanders. While returning from a conference with Oberführer Kurt Meyer, commander of the 12th SS Panzer Division on July 17th, Rommel was severely wounded when his staff car was shot up by Spitfire pilots from the 602 Squadron and crashed into a tree. Ironically, in a twist of fate, the nearby village where Rommel was first treated was called St Foy-de-Montgomery.

Only the day before Rommel had reported to von Kluge that up to July 15th the German Seventh Army Group had lost over 97,000 men and over 250 tanks. Replacements, however, had amounted to only 6,000 personnel and 17 tanks. Ammunition, too, was running short. By comparison, the British, even after the debacle of Goodwood, were able to resupply their forward units within thirty-six hours. The Germans were slowly losing their battle of attrition.

CIRCUIT FIVE

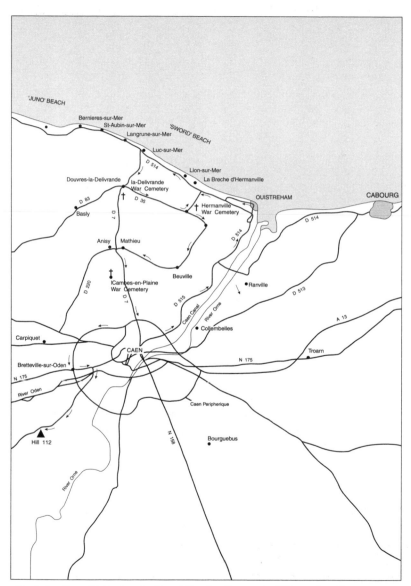

Circuit five. Caen (Ouistreham) – Sword Beach – Douvres-La-Déliverande – Caen

S WORD BEACH STARTS AT OUISTREHAM and runs west to include Luc-sur-Mer. It is divided into four sections, east to west, codenamed: Roger, Queen, Peter, and Oboe. This tour starts in Ouistreham by taking the D-515 from Caen, onto the D-514, and then taking the third exit in the roundabout/rotary (in the center of which is one of the eleven stone monuments erected by the Comité du Débarquement in commemoration of the D-Day landings) and driving into the center of Ouistreham up to the church. Damaged during the fighting, the eleventh-century church had its stained glass windows replaced after the war. One window is dedicated to the Commandos of No. 1 Special Service Brigade, who liberated Ouistreham, and a second window is dedicated to the 51st Highland Division.

Continue from the church toward the sea front and park in the car park adjacent to the casino. This casino was built on the site of the German strongpoint attacked and captured by Commandant Philippe Kieffer and No. 10 (Inter-Allied) French Commandos. Before becoming a German strongpoint, another casino had stood on this site until it was destroyed by Allied bombers in 1942 (hence the reason the German position was referred to as the casino).

Approximately 250 meters west of the casino is a memorial to Commandant Kieffer and the French Commandos on the top of a sand dune. This aluminium sculpture is sited on top of a steel armored cupola and represents the bows of a ship hitting the German defenses. Leading up to the memorial, on either side, are eleven stones that bear the names of those French commandos killed during the liberation of Riva Bella; each of the seven steps you need to climb represents a commando who fell between this memorial and the casino.

Opposite the casino there is the Musée No. 4 Commando. This museum tells the story of the commando's involvement in the D-Day landings and has a selection of documents, weapons, uniforms, and badges on display.

Walk eastward, toward the car ferry, and on your right you will see a fifty-two-foot concrete tower set back from the road, behind the houses. This is the five-level flak tower that was used by the Germans as the local headquarters and is Le Grand Bunker, Musée du Mur d' Atlantique. The Atlantic Wall Museum has been restored to operational condition as it was in 1944. Inside all the rooms are set out with their equipment and there is also the opportunity to operate the range finder that the Germans used to scan the horizon for enemy activity. A selection of photographs and an audio-visual presentation explain the construction of the Atlantic Wall and also how the French resistance supplied the Allies with valuable intelligence about the German defenses.

Return to your car and drive west along the coast road. On entering Colleville-Montgomery-Plage take the next main road turning left and then take a right onto the D-514. On your left you will pass a memorial and statue to Field Marshal (General during the Normandy landings) Sir Bernard Law Montgomery. Continue along the D-514 into La Brèche d'Hermanville and, on your right, are the landing beaches where the first troops of the British 3rd Infantry Division came ashore. As mentioned in the Getting There (pp 14-17) section, it will be worth your while stopping, periodically, along the beaches to search for memorials and other interesting places connected with the D-Day landing. You will not be disappointed at how much there is to find.

Along the D-514 you will see one of "Hobart's Funnies," a Petard tank, which was one of the many names given to a host of weird and wonderful armored vehicles designed by and named after the commanding officer of the 79th Armored Division, Major General Sir Percy Hobart. Hobart's Funnies were also referred to by their generic title as AVREs (Armored Vehicles Royal Engineers) and were divided into two main types: One was the DD or duplex drive tank, which was a Sherman tank fitted with twin propellers, a waterproofed underside, and a collapsible canvas screen that would allow the tank to float and be propelled in calm seas. Upon reaching the beach the drive would be switched to its tracks, the canvas screen dropped, and the tank would roll forward straight into battle.

The second type was given a whole range of names and tasks: the Crocodile was a flame-throwing Churchill tank (see Chapter 6). A Crab, or Flail, tank was a Sherman tank with rotating flails used to clear minefields. A Bobbin was a Churchill tank that carried 100 yards of coconut coil matting on a giant spool above the vehicle; the matting was laid out over soft ground to allow itself and other vehicles to pass over without becoming bogged down. An Armored Ramp Carrier (ARC) was fitted with a mobile ramp that could provide a quick and easy advance over beach walls, ditches, or steams. The Petard, mentioned above, was a Churchill tank with its standard gun replaced by a 290mm short-barrelled mortar. This fired an explosive charge, known as a "flying dustbin," that was used to destroy enemy concrete fortifications.

Continue along the D-514 through Lion-sur-Mer, where No. 41

Commando landed, to Luc-sur-Mer. On the right is a memorial to one of the many small scale commando raids that took place in 1941 (see Chapter 4). Take the last turning left in Luc-sur-Mer, before the sign for Langrune-sur-Mer, onto the D-83 and drive through the village to Douvres-la-Délivrande. On the right as you near the end of the village is the Douvres Radar Station. After several attempts to capture the site by Canadian and British troops, No. 41 Commando, with support provided by the AVRE tanks of the 26th Assault Squadron, Royal Engineers, managed to overpower the German garrison on June 11th. Today the Musée Radar Douvres has exhibits showing in detail the construction of the bunkers and how the radar station was put to use by the Germans.

Return to Douvres-la-Délivrande on the D-83 and take a right onto the D-7, signposted Caen. About 600 meters on your left is la Délivrande War Cemetery (look for the green and white Commonwealth War Graves Commission sign). This cemetery has 1,123 burials, of which 927 are British, 180 German, 11 Canadian, 3 Australian, and 1 Polish. The first casualties buried here are from the Peter and Oboe sectors of Sword Beach and were killed on D-Day. A Royal Army Medical Corps operating theater was set up at the convent in la Délivrande during the Normandy campaign and the other bodies that rest here come from the fighting between the beaches and Caen. As with all the Commonwealth War Cemeteries, a register and plan of the cemetery can be found in one of the stone shelters in the cemetery grounds.

Head back toward the church in Douvres-la-Délivrande and take a right turn onto the D-35, heading for Hermanville-sur-Mer and Colleville-Montgomery. Turn left into Hermanville-sur-Mer, onto the D-60, and then take a right in the village just after the Mairie (Town Hall). 300 meters on your right is Hermanville War Cemetery. Of the 1,005 burials, 986 are British, 13 are Canadian, 3 are Australian, and 3 are French. Most of these were killed during the first few days of the landings.

Return to the D-35 and drive into Colleville-Montgomery. On the right is the site of the German fortification known as Hillman. A narrow road called "Rue du Suffolk Regiment" leads up to the bunkers and memorial. The memorial, placed on the side of the bunker, is dedicated to the 1st Battalion Suffolk Regiment. A plaque gives further details of the site and battle as well as a panoramic table that shows the extent of the Hillman defenses.

From Hillman continue along the narrow road until you reach Beuville. Turn right onto the D-141, through Beuville, and head for

Mathieu. Turn left onto the D-220 and then left again onto the D-7. When you reach La Bijude, turn right, onto the D-79b, and then take the next right, onto the D-220a, heading for Anisy. After a few kilometers, Cambes-en-Plaine War Cemetery will be on your left. This cemetery contains 224 burials, all British, of which the majority are from the South Staffordshire and North Staffordshire Regiments, killed in the fighting for Caen between July 8th and 9th.

Return to the D-7 and turn right heading for Caen. Turn right onto the "périphérique" and follow the signs for the memorial. Built on the site of a German command post, this museum and memorial is divided into seven sections: 1) "Failure of peace;" 2) "The pre-war years and rise of Hitler;" 3) "France during the dark years;" 4) "The World War;" 5) "Landings of June 6th 1944;" 6) "The Battle of Normandy;" and 7) "Hope," which tells of other major events since World War Two and the efforts of international organizations to promote peace around the world.

This modern museum also has a library, which is open to all visitors, a restaurant, a well-stocked shop, and even a free childcare service to keep the younger children occupied while their parents give their attention to the memorial's exhibits. Please note that at least half a day is required to view the memorial.

From the memorial continue counter-clockwise around the "périphérique" and exit for Bretteville-sur-Odon. Take the N-175, heading for the center of Caen and then take a right onto the D-8. Follow the D-8 out toward Évrecy, and on your left there is Hill 112. Nearby there is a monument to 43rd Wessex Division and also a monument to the Dorset and Hampshire Regiments.

From here, the quickest way back to Caen is to return via the route you have just taken.

6

GOLD BEACH TO BLUECOAT

FROM SIX-AN-A-HALF MILES OFFSHORE, the landing crafts of the British 50th (Northumbrian) Division, under the command of XXX Corps, were lowered into the stormy waters of the English Channel. The flat-bottomed boats yawed and bucked through white-topped waves while cold and seasick soldiers huddled inside. Preceding the troops were the crews of the DD (duplex drive) tanks; unlike their American counterparts, the DD tanks' first battle would not be with natural elements. Their commanders had decided not to risk immersing the waterproofed tanks into the turbulent sea. Instead, the armor was carried by the landing craft right onto the beach. Additionally, the tanks were supported by Hobart's Funnies and Royal Engineer demolition parties whose task was clearing the formidable beach obstacles.

The midnight bombing raids had silenced two of the three German coastal batteries along Gold Beach, at Ver-sur-Mer and Mont Fleury. A third battery at Longues, however, southwest of Arromanches, had survived the 1,000 tons of bombs dropped throughout the night. Its 152mm guns, with their range of twenty kilometers, began firing at an American cruiser the USS Arkansas, and a destroyer that were anchored off Omaha Beach just as the Allies began their pre–dawn naval bombardment.

The USS Arkansas, supported by two French destroyers George-Leygues and Montcalm, returned fire and after a brief exchange, the battery redirected its aim toward the fleet anchored off Gold Beach. Shells whistled perilously close to the headquarters ship HMS Bulolo, forcing it to move position. The HMS Ajax immediately returned fire with its own 152mm guns. After a twenty-minute duel, in which time over 100 rounds were fired at the coastal guns, the German battery fell silent.

On the right flank of the beach landings, between Le Hamel and Asnelles, the troops of the 231st Brigade were greeted by heavy fire.

1st Battalion, The Hampshires and 1st Battalion, The Dorsets, were the first infantry troops to come ashore, followed immediately by No. 47 (RM) Commando. The brigade eventually secured the villages and began their push westward to link up with the American troops on Omaha Beach. The 1st Hampshire Regiment captured Arromanches, the area where the British Mulberry harbor would be built, while No. 47 (RM) Commando pushed on along the coast line to its objective of Port-en-Bessin, the site of PLUTO (Pipe Line under the Ocean). This small fishing port also marked the dividing line between the British and American sectors.

The commandos had already suffered heavy losses when four of their LCAs were sunk while coming ashore. In addition, strong German defenses over the thirteen kilometers to Port-en-Bessin held up their advance until the evening and consequently the commandos were unable to liberate the port until the following day. This began after a pre-assault naval bombardment was laid down and rocket-firing Typhoon fighter aircraft had attempted to soften up the German defenses. The commandos' attack was particularly hazardous because of the series of bunkers and trenches in the high cliffs on either side of the port. The commandos lost nearly half their men during the assault, which was also

The Lounges Battery. A young visitor gives an idea of the scale.

subjected to fire from the German flak (anti-aircraft) boats moored in the harbor, but they eventually succeeded in liberating Port-en-Bessin by nightfall on June 7th and capturing the garrison commander.

During the afternoon of D-Day the Germans had managed to get the massive naval guns of the Lounges battery back into action. By shelling the American troops on Omaha Beach, they further hindered the American's already perilously slow progress. Again the *USS Arkansas* along with the two French destroyers, *George-Leygues* and *Montcalm*, pounded the battery into submission and eventually the Germans surrendered to the advancing British troops later that evening without a fight.

On the left flank of Gold Beach, the 69th Infantry Brigade launched its initial assault with an attack onto the beaches just west of La Rivière. Here the 5th Battalion of the East Yorkshires attacked the easternmost part of the beach and made their way through the Mont Fleury Battery toward Ver-sur-Mer. Meanwhile, the 6th Battalion, Green Howards landed further to the east.

EYEWITNESS

When we landed the doors opened, we jumped out, but there were no bullets. The Beach was apparently deserted . . . . At every step we expected to be fired at, but we were not. The lack of opposition became eerie. Then, after about 200 yards, we must have reached a German fixed line for suddenly they threw everything at us. The mortars took us first and I was hit badly in the leg. My radio operator and policeman were both killed outright by the explosion.

Major RJL Jackson, beachmaster, 6th Battalion, Green Howards

As the Green Howards made their way off the beach, toward the Mont Fleury battery, a company commander noticed that two German pillboxes had been missed during the initial assault. Accompanied by Company Sergeant Major Stan Hollis, he went to investigate. As they approached a muzzle flash lit up from inside the darkened slit of the pillbox. CSM Hollis immediately charged straight at the pillbox firing his Sten gun into the slit. He jumped on top of the concrete bunker and reloaded his weapon. Crouching down he threw a grenade through the doorway. Following the explosion, before the dust had settled, he fired his Sten into the pillbox.

Two Germans were killed outright and the rest surrendered. Hollis then continued to advance along a neighboring communications trench and succeeded in gathering over twenty prisoners.

As the Green Howards made their way inland into the village of Crépon, Hollis was put in command of a party to cover an attack on a German field gun and machine-gun nest. When his cover party was held up during the advance Hollis decided, wanting to waste no more time, to take on the gun crew himself. Armed with a PIAT (infantry anti-tank weapon, equivalent to the American bazooka) he moved forward with his men. As they moved into a nearby house, a German sniper fired and grazed Hollis's right cheek; at the same time the German field gun swung round and fired a shot into the building where Hollis and his men were taking shelter. To avoid the falling debris he moved his men to an alternative position. By this time the German gun crew had already taken casualties and soon after the gun was destroyed.

It was later discovered that two of his men had been left behind in the damaged house, in full view from the German positions. Hollis immediately volunteered to rescue them and went, alone, toward the German lines. With a Bren gun he was able to distract the Germans while his men made their way back to safety under the cover of his diversion. For his heroic and selfless actions, which undoubtedly saved the lives of many of his men, CSM Stan Hollis later received Britain's highest decoration for gallantry, the Victoria Cross – the only one to be awarded for action on D-Day itself, a day which witnessed many acts of gallantry from many men of many nationalities.

By nightfall, the 50th Northumbrian Division and 8th Armored Brigade had created and were holding their own bridgehead. In total, over 25,000 men held a line twelve kilometers wide along the Gold Beach sector, stretching from Arromanches and Courseulles, and up to fourteen kilometers deep, from the beaches to the main Bayeux-Caen Road (now the N-13). Contact had also been established with the Canadians from Juno Beach, but it was uncertain what had happened to the Americans on Omaha Beach. Recce patrols managed to penetrate the town of Bayeux just before midnight and the following day Bayeux was liberated without much of a fight. Since the majority of the German troops had been moved out toward the Cherbourg Peninsula, to join in the fighting against the American airborne troops, the town was spared the destruction that had, and would, befall so many other towns during the battle for Normandy. Since the ancient streets of Bayeux had not been designed for large military

One of the Tiger tanks of the 12th SS (Hitler Jugend) Panzer Division.

vehicles, the Royal Engineers began construction of a ring road around the town. In the weeks that followed, Bayeux was turned into a major supply and hospital base.

By June 7th, the Bayeux-Caen highway was in the hands of XXX Corps and so, too, was the main railway line. With Rommel's panzer units having been deployed in the defense of Caen, the only armored resistance the Germans could offer in this area was a reconnaissance battalion of the 12th Panzer SS (Hitler Jugend). Unfortunately, the build-up of supplies was falling behind schedule so Lieutenant General Miles Dempsey, commander of the British, decided not to risk overstretching his supply lines. He dug-in on the high ground south and southeast of Bayeux

The following day the British advance continued heading through the Bocage toward Tilly-sur-Seulles. General Dollmann ordered Bayerlein's Panzer (Lehr) Division toward the village in order to hold the line but moving the armor in daylight proved to be a big mistake, as squadrons of

Typhoons were constantly on the prowl behind the German lines with orders to disrupt any enemy movement.

Despite the losses the German had managed to make their defense lines south of Tilly-sur-Seulles and were building up their supplies in order to launch a three-division attack: east of Caen, the 21st Panzer

EYEWITNESS

My men were calling the main road from Vire to Le Bény Bocage Jabo-Rennstrecke [Fighter-bomber racecourse] . . . . By the end of the day I had lost forty petrol wagons and ninety other trucks. Five of my tanks had been knocked out, as well as eighty-four half-tracks, prime movers and S.P. guns. These losses were serious for a division not yet in action.
General Fritz Bayerlein, commander, Panzer Lehr Division

A camouflaged Tiger tank near Villers-Bocage.

Division would take the right flank; between Caen and Fontenay-le-Pesnel in the center, the 12th SS (Hitler Jugend) Panzer Division would attack; and, on the left flank, the Panzer (Lehr) Division would move between Fontenay-le-Pesnel and Hottot-les-Bagues.

This land, south of Bayeux, was ideal defensive country. The high hedgerows and small fields of the Bocage were now combined with undulating hills and thickening woodland that provided ideal cover. The well-concealed German panther tanks with their heavy armor and superior armament proved too much for the thinly armored Sherman tanks. What the Germans had to fear, though, was the British artillery and undisputed air superiority. Rocket-firing Typhoons, naval, and field-gun bombardments kept the German offensive in check.

On the afternoon of June 8th, General von Geyr, commander of the Panzer troops in the West, decided that the full-scale attack should take place, under the cover of darkness, on June 10th or 11th. But before the Germans had a chance to launch their assault, the British and Canadians put in their own attack. To the west, the Americans were also closing in. The German commanders were immediately put onto the defensive. The British plan, codenamed Operation Perch, was for the "Desert Rats" of the British 7th Armored Division to attack south of Bayeux, then bypass the German armor and head southeast toward Villers-Bocage.

The capture of Caen was the main priority of the 51st Highlanders. The division would launch its attack east of Caen and drive southward. If the initial assault proved successful, then the British 1st Airborne Division, still in reserve in England, would drop south of the city and complete the envelopment of Caen. The success of this operation, however, depended on the Desert Rats taking and holding the high ground and road junction at Villers-Bocage.

Initially, the leading force of the 22nd Armored Brigade attempted to breach the Panzer (Lehr) defense line near Tilly-sur-Seulles, but two days of fighting resulted in an advance of only three miles. Lieutenant General Dempsey, British Second Army Commander, redirected the armor to take a right hook, bypassing the German armor and heading directly for Villers-Bocage. All started well and the 22nd managed to reach the village, via Caumont, almost without opposition. Led by the eccentric Brigadier Robert "Loony" Hinde, British tanks drove into the village and continued on toward their objective, Hill 213, which was one kilometer to the northeast along the highway to Caen (N-175). It looked as though Monty's plan was about to work but before the infantry of 50th (Northumbrian) Division had a chance to consolidate the gains, a tank-busting ace of the 12th SS Panzer Division would, almost singlehandedly, thwart the British advance.

Thirty-year-old Lieutenant Michel Wittmann, commanding a Panzer Tiger company of the Hitler Youth division, had already been awarded the Laurel Leaves to the Knight's Cross he had won for his action in Russia, where he had destroyed over 100 Russian tanks. As Wittmann made his way toward the hill near the village with a small unit of less than half a dozen tanks, he witnessed scores of British armored vehicles racing along the Caen road late in the morning of June 13th. With his trusted driver, Corporal Böll, Wittmann systematically began to pick off the British halftracks and Cromwell tanks. Return fire from the Cromwell tanks was no threat to the heavily armored Panzer VIE Tiger tanks, so soon the burning wrecks of over twenty-seven British tanks and other armored vehicles littered the roadway. Brigadier Hinde ordered the remnants of his brigade back into the village. Wittmann gave chase to the retreating British troops and with the support of more German tanks he entered the village.

Newly-promoted Haupsturmführer Michel Wittmann after the battle at Villers-Bocage.

The aftermath of Wittmann's attack.

Here the British troops stood their ground and by 1600, the German counter-offensive had been beaten off with the loss of over half a dozen German tanks. This included Wittmann's own Tiger, which had its track blown off by a PIAT. Wittmann managed to escape both injury and capture and, because of his action, was awarded the Oak Leaves on his Knight's Cross. He was also promoted to Hauptsturmführer (Captain).

Less than a month later his luck ran out against an overwhelming force of Canadian Shermans during the fighting south of Caen. Wittmann took out three of the Canadian tanks before he was eventually surrounded and killed when his own tank was destroyed. His body was buried in a shallow grave by the side of the road where it would remain, undiscovered, for nearly forty years. (Found in 1983, his remains were laid to rest in the massive German Cemetery at La Cambe with 20,000 other German soldiers. The burial was attended by surviving veterans of 12th SS Panzer).

One of the Cromwell tanks destroyed by Wittman.

With his advance halted, and under attack from fresh German reinforcements, Hinde decided he had to consolidate his defenses and withdraw his force to Hill 174, two kilometers west of Villers-Bocage. He would hold this high ground until relieved by the infantry from the 50th Division. But instead of reinforcing Hinde's position, higher authority ordered another attack against the German lines at Tilly-sur-Seulles. Despite concentrated air support, the Panzer (Lehr) could not be moved and held its ground. By noon the following day, the 7th Armored Division was pulled back to Briquessard, two miles east of Caumont. Though the operation had failed, the British Second Army's aggressive offensive had served two purposes: 1) it had protected the left flank of the American First Army, as it continued to secure the Cherbourg Peninsula and the Brittany ports; and 2) it had kept the might of the German panzer divisions on the defensive. The longer these divisions were distracted, the sooner the whole Allied bridgehead could be expanded. Unfortunately it also meant that Caen could now only be taken in a series of set piece attacks.

It had become a war of attrition, with the Germans having committed all their armored forces and with the British desperately trying to build up their own. The close quarter fighting in the Bocage had taken a terrible toll in men and vehicles, but Tilly-sur-Seulles eventually fell on June 18th. On the next day a major disaster stuck the Allied armies.

With over half a million men to feed and over 100,000 vehicles to keep supplied and moving, the vast army had only enough rations to last them about seven days. On June 19th, Normandy suffered its worst storm in living memory. The two artificial harbors codenamed Mulberry A, on Omaha Beach, and Mulberry B, at Arromanches, were severely damaged during the storm. Monty had to postpone his planned offensive until the storm abated and supplies could once again be brought ashore. Three days later, when the storm had passed, the damage was assessed. In total 800 vessels had been damaged or destroyed. Landing craft littered the beaches and the Mulberry harbors were in complete disarray. It was decided that the American harbor at Omaha should be scrapped and used to repair the Mulberry at Arromanches since this harbor, positioned in a natural cove, had suffered the least damage. While this was being done, the Allies had to rely upon their supplies being brought ashore directly onto the beaches or into the small fishing ports that dot the Calvados and La Manche coastline.

A British Bren gun carrier.

While the Canadians and British troops began their set piece attacks to capture Caen, the next major offensive in the Bocage country was Operation Bluecoat. This was intended to relieve the pressure on the American Operation Cobra, which had been designed to open up the gap between the two German Army groups. On July 31st the Operation Bluecoat attack was launched south, from Caumont, by XXX Corps supported by VIII Corps. The British troops were tasked with a push eastward, through Villers-Bocage, to take the western half of the Mont Pinçon Ridge as well as a push southward toward Vire. This operation would cover Lieutenant General Omar Bradley's First Army flank and allow the Americans to exploit their gains by sweeping around toward Falaise.

Despite the concentration of German armor now diverted to defend Caen, the fighting was still hard since the Germans had been given time to prepare their defenses. VIII Corps had managed to take part of the ridge by August 1st but XXX Corps was struggling and didn't take Villers-Bocage until the 4th. Further south, a reconnaissance troop of the 11th Armored Division had, on July 31st, been able to take a road bridge over the River Souleuvre (on the D-56). Situated in a ravine, several reconnaissance tanks were able to cross over the bridge before their advance was checked by the Germans. With the bridge safely crossed and in British hands, the advance was able to continue later that day when reinforcements arrived. (It was discovered after the war that the bridge, on the demarcation line between the German Seventh Army and Panzer

Group West (later called the Fifth Panzer Army), had been left undefended by the two army commanders since each thought it came under the other's control).

EYEWITNESS

For us the Mont Pinçon operation was a bitter and fruitless day before St. Jean le Blanc, the withdrawal following it, and then an equally bitter battle to reach and hold the summit; not a battle against the Germans, so much as against the burning sun, the choking dust, our parched throats and empty bellies, the craggy slopes and tangled thickets, the rocky earth and above all our utterly weary bodies.

Major A. Parsons, company commander, 4th Wiltshire Regiment

As the Germans withdrew from Villers-Bocage and the area around Aunay-sur-Odon, north of Mont Pinçon, they left, in their wake, a network of booby-traps and demolished buildings. The battle at Mont Pinçon began on August 5th, under the command of XXX Corps' newly appointed commander, Lieutenant General Horrocks. It was a costly and arduous battle that fluctuated back and forth around the nearby villages and fields until eventually the German resolve was broken and the

exhausted British troops managed to clamber up the steep rugged slopes to the top. It was not just fighting the Germans that made the men tire; the weather and terrain, too, proved to be as much of a burden.

Further south, near Vire, the battles were equally hard and costly. In one, near Pavée, Corporal Sidney "Basher" Bates, almost single-handedly, saved his unit of the 1st Battalion, The Royal Norfolk Regiment, while being attacked by an almost overwhelming force of German SS panzer grenadiers. Bates selflessly counterattacked with a Bren gun. His citation tells the story:

British PIAT Team.

Citation of Victoria Cross
CORPORAL SIDNEY BATES
aged 23 years, of 'B' Company 1st Battalion, The Royal Norfolk Regiment

The attack in strength by 10th SS Panzer Division near Sourdevalle* started with a heavy and accurate artillery and mortar programme on the position which the enemy had, by this time, pinpointed. Half an hour later the main attack developed and heavy machine-gun and mortar fire was concentrated on the point of a junction of the two forward companies. Corporal Bates was commanding the right forward section of the left forward company which suffered some casualties, so he decided to move the remnants of his section to an alternative position whence he appreciated he could better counter the enemy thrust.

However, the enemy wedge grew still deeper, until there were about 50 to 60 Germans, supported by machine-guns and mortars, in the area occupied by the section.

Seeing that the situation was becoming desperate, Corporal Bates then seized a light machine gun and charged the enemy, moving forward through a hail of bullets and splinters and firing the gun from the hip. He was almost immediately wounded by machine gun fire and fell to the ground, but recovering himself quickly, he got up and continued advancing toward the enemy, spraying bullets from his gun as he went. His action was now having an effect on the enemy riflemen and machine gunners, but the mortar bombs continued to fall around him.

He was then hit a second time, and much more seriously and painfully wounded. Undaunted, he staggered once more to his feet and continued toward the enemy, who were now seemingly nonplussed at their inability to check him. His constant firing continued until the enemy started to withdraw before him. At this moment he was hit for the third time by mortar-bomb splinters and sustained a wound that would prove fatal. He fell to the ground but continued firing until his strength failed him. This was not, however, until the enemy had withdrawn and the situation in this locality had been restored.

Left, Sydney Bates, VC and above, Sydney Bates's headstone in Bayeux War Cemetery.

* *Though the Victoria Cross citation states Sourdevalle, the action actually took place in a field near Pavée.*

Desperately wounded, Corporal Bates was stretchered back to a nearby Regimental Aid Post. He died of his wounds two days later on August 8th. He was posthumously awarded the Victoria Cross for his action and is now buried in Bayeux War Cemetery. (The Royal Norfolk Regiment had the highest number of recipients of the VC during World War Two, with a total of five awards.)

Despite the cost, Operation Bluecoat had been a success and had given the Americans time to widen their corridor and allow the First Army to push its bridgehead south and east. Only the Mortain counter-attack on August 7th posed any threat, but this was soon stopped by Allied air superiority. The Germans were once again on the retreat.

EYEWITNESS

We made a swift advance of about ten miles and suffered only three tank losses . . . . Suddenly the Allied fighter-bombers swooped out of the sky. They came down in hundreds firing their rockets at concentrated tanks and vehicles. We could do nothing against them, and we could make no further progress. The next day the planes came down again. We were forced to give the ground we had gained, and by the 9th August the division was back where it had started from north of Montain, having lost thirty tanks and eight hundred men."
Generaloberst Heinrich von Lüttwitz, GOC, XLVII Panzer Corps

Now it was a matter of keeping up the momentum and – with the help of the British and Canadian offensives from Sword and Juno Beach and the 6th Airborne Division east of the River Orne – of trapping the Germans in the Falaise Pocket. If this tactic was successful, Hitler would lose much of his retreating army and it was hoped that the morale of his remaining soldiers would be severely reduced thereby shortening, still further, the length of the war in northwest Europe.

CIRCUIT SIX

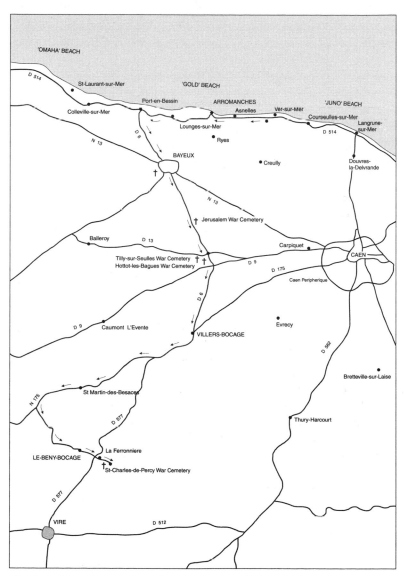

Circuit six. Caen – Arromanches – Bayeux – Lounges – Tilly-sur-Seulles – Caen

Gold Beach starts just west of Courseulles at Ver-sur-Mer (also known as La Rivière). Driving east on the D-514 coastal highway from Ouistreham, Gold Beach is divided into three sections, codenamed King, Jig, and Item. As you drive through Ver-sur-Mer you are passing the point at which the 5th Battalion, East Yorkshire Regiment landed. Further on, just before the crossroads, is a house that was used by Admiral Sir Bertram Ramsay, commander in chief of the Naval Forces, as his HQ during the Normandy Campaign. A plaque on the right-hand gate pillar commemorates this fact. Immediately after the crossroads, on the right, is a memorial to the Royal Artillery regiments that were attached to the 50th Northumbrian Division. As you continue along the D-514, the next crossroads is where the 6th Battalion, Green Howards landed. The narrow road to your right, leading to the beach, was used by them as their beach exit. To your left, the road leads to the former site of the Mont Fleury Battery. This can be found by taking the third right along the road and going down a narrow track. Little remains, though, of the battery itself and throughout the summer the field is fenced off to prevent anyone from disturbing the farmer's crops. A far better example of a German battery can be seen later in this tour at Lounges-sur-Mer.

Continue along the D-514, which runs parallel to the open marshland and beach. If you look out to sea, you will be able to see the unmistakable concrete caissons of the Mulberry Harbor. As you pass through Asnelles and Le Hamel you can see where the first two Battalions of the 231st Brigade landed, followed by No. 47 (RM) Commando, who went on to take Port-en-Bessin. The road then climbs up toward St Côme-de-Fresné, which overlooks Arromanches from the east. Park in the parking lot at the top and take a look at the orientation platform which uses diagrams to show the size and scale of the Mulberry Harbor. Also at St Côme-de-Fresné there is an excellent cinema called the "Arromanches 360." The film shown is called "The Price of Freedom" and is projected onto nine screens in a circular hall. There is no commentary, only stunning images of archive footage carefully edited into scenes of a present day Normandy. There can be no better way to envision the intensity and sheer scale of the Normandy landings than to be immersed for twenty minutes in this remarkable 360 degree film show.

Along the cliff top at St Côme-de-Fresné is a memorial to the Royal Engineers, as well as the remnants of the German bunkers and gun emplacements. The German defenses here consisted of two 77mm and three anti-aircraft guns. These were overpowered on the afternoon of D-Day after a naval bombardment by *HMS Belfast,* the 11,500 ton cruiser that is now open to the public at its mooring on the River Thames in London. With these defenses destroyed, the troops of 1st Battalion, The Hampshire Regiment, with a tank squadron in support, were able to continue with their advance into Arromanches.

Drive down into Arromanches. On the front, next to the parking lot, is the Musée du Débarquement. This museum is a permanent exhibition and memorial to the D-Day landings. Inside the design and construction of the Mulberry Harbor is explained in detail using models and exhibits. It also goes on to explain the importance of the harbor during the invasion of Normandy with a slide and film show. Arromanches is a pleasant coastal resort that offers a good selection of restaurants and souvenir shops for the Battlefield Tourist.

From Arromanches follow the signs for Bayeux along the D-514 and follow the sign, on your right, for the Batterie de Longues. Follow this road (still the D-514), through Tracy-sur-Mer and Manvieux, until you reach Lounges-sur-Mer. Turn right down the D-104 until you come to the Lounges Battery. This is probably the best example of a German coastal battery in Normandy. The four reinforced concrete casemates have been preserved and restored, complete with 155mm naval guns. In one casemate there are only the remnants of a destroyed gun, in the other three, the impressive guns stand as if they are still ready for action. A walk down to the cliff edge will take you to the observation post. Two floors high, it is set into the cliff edge and in 1944 was protected by anti-aircraft guns, a 20mm cannon, and searchlights. The solid reinforced concrete bunker also had underground telephone cables running to each of the casemates.

Return from Lounges, and take a right onto the D-514. Continue through Marigny and Commes then, after entering Port-en-Bessin, turn right and go down to the parking lot on the harbor. On the eastern side of the harbor, at the base of the cliff, a memorial to No. 47 (RM) Commando was erected on an old German bunker. Just above this is an old seventeenth-century Vauban tower. Beyond this, at the top of the cliff, an extensive network of communication trenches and German bunkers remains. Across the other side of the harbor, on the western cliff, more evidence of the German defenses can be found. Port-en-Bessin represented the demarcation line between the British and

American sector. It is, however, most famous for its siting as the continental terminal of PLUTO, the "Pipe Line under the Ocean" that ran from Sandown and Shanklin on the Isle of Wight, beneath the English Channel, and into Port-en-Bessin. In fact there were four 150mm pipelines: one each for petrol, oil, and water plus a reserve pipeline in case one of the others was damaged. The pipeline was completed and in working order by June 25th. A week later, a second terminal was constructed in the American sector at St Honorine. Between the two terminals, over 7,000 tons of fuel were brought ashore to the fighting armies each day.

On leaving Port-en-Bessin take the D-6 signposted Bayeux. Approximately one kilometer along the road, on the left, is the Musée des Épaves Sous-marines du Débarquement [Museum of D-Day Wrecks]. This museum displays a selection of military equipment that has been salvaged by underwater exploration off the D-Day landing beaches. As well as large military vehicles, like tanks, landing craft, and artillery, many personal effects have also been discovered and are now on display as a testament to the sacrifice of those who were killed in the battle for Normandy.

Continue along the D-6 to Bayeux, turn left on the main ring road around Bayeux and follow the road around until you come to the

A Normandy veteran visits old comrades at the Bayeux War Cemetery.

Commonwealth War Graves Commission Cemetery on your right. Parking spaces are provided in front of the cemetery gates. Bayeux War Cemetery is the largest of all the World War Two cemeteries in France with 4,648 graves. Most are British (3,935 graves), while the rest are

made up of: 466 Germans, 181 Canadian, 25 Polish, 17 Australian, 8 New Zealanders, 7 Russians, 3 French, 2 Czechs, 2 Italians, 1 South African, and 1 unidentified. The names of all these can be found in the cemetery register situated in the small stone building on the left of the cemetery. Among those buried here are Corporal Stanley Bates who was awarded the Victoria Cross.

Directly across the road from the cemetery is the Bayeux Memorial. On this are engraved the names of the 1,808 men of the commonwealth forces who fell in the Battle for Normandy and who have no known grave. Among those names are 189

The Bayeux Memorial.

men from the 43rd Divisional Reconnaissance Regiment who had been aboard the ill-fated *Derry Cunihy*. This ship was anchored off the coast of Ouistreham, on the night of July 23rd, awaiting a chance for the men aboard to disembark. That night there was the usual activity from German aircraft who regularly flew over the channel dropping mines. The next morning at 0800 when the ship's engines were started, disaster struck. The engine noise detonated a submerged mine and the ship's hull was ripped apart. As the ship sank in minutes, the men below decks didn't stand a chance. At roll call that evening 150 men were confirmed wounded; a further 189 were listed as missing. It is these men who now have their names immortalized in the white stone of the Bayeux Memorial. The Latin epitaph along the frieze of this memorial makes reference to William the Bastard's (Conqueror) invasion of England in 1066. The translation reads: "We, once conquered by William, have now set free the Conqueror's native land."

From the cemetery continue along the road for about 200 meters and turn left into the parking lot of the Musée Memorial de la Bataille de Normandie. This museum has information and exhibits relating to the whole of the Normandy campaign. On display is the largest selection of uniforms, small arms, photographs, documents, and other military equipment in Normandy and is well worth a visit. The museum also has toilets, a small selection of refreshments, and a bookstall. Among the exhibits outside are a German Hetzer, a Sherman tank, and one of Hobart's Funnies – a flame-throwing Churchill "Crocodile" tank.

From the Battle of Normandy Museum in Bayeux, continue along the ring road and take the third exit right, the D-6 signposted Tilly-sur-Seulles. After eight kilometers, on the left hand side of the road, is the smallest World War Two Commonwealth Cemetery in France. Called Jérusalem, named after the small hamlet near Chouain, this cemetery has only forty-seven burials. The cemetery was started on June 10th, 1944 with the burials of three men from the Durham Light Infantry. Nearly half of those buried here come from that same regiment. This area was part of the battlefield that witnessed vicious counterattacks by the German panzer divisions who sought to retake Bayeux.

From Jérusalem continue along the D-6 until you reach Tilly-sur-Seulles. In the center of the village take a right at the main crossroads onto the D-13. One kilometer on the left hand side is Tilly-sur-Seulles War Cemetery. The village of Tilly-sur-Seulles was taken and lost a total of twenty-two times between June 7th and 18th in battles between the

Panzer (Lehr) and the 49th and 50th Infantry Divisions and the 7th Armored Division. After the village was taken for the twenty-third time, it remained in British hands though the battles continued, and casualties mounted, well into July. This cemetery is one of two in the area that contains the dead of those bloody and costly battles. There are 1,222 burials here: 986 British, 322 Germans, 2 New Zealanders, 1 Canadian, and 1 Australian.

Return to Tilly-sur-Seulles and turn right back onto the D-6. On the right, in the Chapel of Notre Dame du Val, is the Musée de la Bataille de Tilly. This museum has a selection of documents, maps, photographs, and weapons that were found on the battlefield and are now displayed in the now tranquil setting of this twelfth-century chapel.

Return to the D-6 and continue through Tilly-sur-Seulles until you reach the T-junction with the D-9. Turn right and the cemetery of Hottot-les-Bagues is about 600 meters on your right. There are 1,137 burials: 965 British, 132 German, 34 Canadian, 3 Australian, 2 New Zealanders, and 1 South African.

Drive back along the D-9 and take the next right onto the D-6 and continue through Villers-Bocage. Take a right onto the N-175 to St Martin-des-Besaces. In this village is the Musée de la Percee du Bocage. This museum tells the story of how the British broke through the Bocage region in the summer of 1944 and of the liberation of St Martin-des-Besaces by the 11th Armored Division.

Return to the N-175 and continue until you reach the D-56, signposted Le Bény-Bocage, on the left. Follow this road until you reach a small bridge over the River Souleuvre. This is the bridge captured intact by Lieutenant Powle of the 2nd Household Cavalry, 11th Armored Division, which allowed the swift advance into Le Bény-Bocage. Now called "Le Pont du Taureau," a plaque on the bridge commemorates this achievement.

Continue along the D-56, through Le Bény-Bocage and the small hamlet of le Ferronniere. Take the next right and just past the cemetery on the left, park your car. This is the St Charles-de-Percy Commonwealth War Cemetery and the furthest south of all the Normandy War Cemeteries. In the heart of the Bocage country this isolated cemetery is the final resting places of 789 Allied servicemen. Four of the graves are Canadian (including three airmen); the rest are British. Most of the soldiers buried here died during Operation Bluecoat, the offensive of the British Second Army to drive a wedge

D-DAY AND THE BATTLE FOR NORMANDY

between the two German Army groups of 7th Army and Panzer Group West during the period of July 31st to August 7th.

From St Charles-de-Percy you can retrace your route back to Le Ferronniere; then take a right turn onto the D-577. Follow this road to the end and take a right onto N-175. This will take you straight onto the Caen "périphérique" (ring-road). Alternatively, turn off at Villers-Bocage and take the D-6 back into Bayeux.

7
JUNO BEACH TO FALAISE

THE FIRST WAVES OF THE CANADIAN 3RD INFANTRY DIVISION coming ashore on Juno Beach landed on top of, and among, the mined steel beach defenses. The naval commanders had feared an offshore reef might present as great a hazard to the landing craft as did the German defenses, so they delayed the landing by fifteen minutes to 0745. Strong winds and rough seas pushed their assault formations out of position causing many to land even later and, with the tide quickly coming in, they drifted onto the mined obstacles.

The initial landings were on the beaches either side of the Norman coastal port of Courseulles-sur-Mer. Over 300 vessels made their way through the rough seas toward these beaches. Of the twenty-five vessels in the first wave, twenty were destroyed or damaged; by the end of the day another sixty-six had been added to the total. In order to get anywhere near the beach, the landing craft personnel were forced to run their craft, sometimes blind, over rows of underwater mines and steel spiked barriers. Adding to the nightmare was the continuous artillery and mortar fire that sent plumes of sand, shrapnel, and water both skyward and sideward, across the beaches, into the advancing troops. The DD tanks failed to reach shore before the infantry so men had to run over the sand and shingle without any protection.

Courseulles-sur-Mer was one of the most heavily defended positions attacked by the Anglo-Canadian forces that day. There were an 88mm, two 75mm, and two 50mm guns covering the beach area, in addition to twelve concrete machine gun posts and several mortar pits, which were able to direct their fire onto any point along the beach. The Regina Rifle Regiment and 6th Armored Regiment landed on the beach east of the River Seulles. One company landed right in front of a German strongpoint, near the mouth of the river, and was immediately pinned down. The remaining companies landed further east and managed to get off the beach and attack Courseulles-sur-Mer from the east. To the west of the river mouth at Courseulles-sur-Mer, the Royal Winnipeg Rifles also landed in front of a German strongpoint but managed to overpower the defenders when the tanks of the Royal Canadian Engineers arrived. Here the Canadian Scottish also landed and moved inland.

EYEWITNESS

The first thing we saw were bodies, and parts of bodies, our own people [sic] and this country that was strange to us, and all these pillboxes everywhere . . . . I can always remember seeing the steeple of this church, and there were snipers up there zapping us with lead flying all around.
Rifleman G. Suche, The Royal Winnipeg Rifles

Further to the east, at St Aubin-sur-Mer, The North Shore Regiment, supported by the 10th Armored Regiment and Royal Canadian Engineers, landed and managed to capture the local German strongpoints just before noon. They were also assisted by No. 48 (RM) Commando, which landed an hour after the Canadians and fought their way toward Sword Beach. Other British troops in the Canadian sector included the men from the 8th Battalion of the King's Liverpool Regiment who made up the beach group.

The incoming tide was presenting a problem for the troops coming ashore, for the beach area was narrowing even as the number of vehicles and armor increased. While the fighting continued in and around the coastal villages, the follow-up units pressed on inland, as quickly as possible, toward the Canadian Division's objectives. These were a group of villages that sat astride the main Caen-Bayeux highway. Among these villages was their main prize – Carpiquet airfield. With an airfield captured and secured the Allies would be able to increase their supplies and reinforcements into the Normandy bridgehead. The Canadians managed to advance more than eleven kilometers, further than any of the other divisions on D-Day, and had cut off the Caen-Bayeux highway by mid-afternoon. They had also been able to link up with the British 50th Northumbrian Division on their right flank, making a front line that ran for twenty-four kilometers. By nightfall the Canadians had secured a sizable bridgehead, with a loss of about 1,000 men.

Throughout the night, while the front line soldiers fought to maintain their bridgehead, others worked around the clock to insure that the beaches were kept clear and that the build-up of supplies could continue.

Despite the Canadians' swift advance, no contact had yet been established with the British 3rd Infantry Division to their left. As the Canadians and British advanced inland, Hitler's Panzer Divisions launched the first of many counterattacks in an attempt to exploit the gap in the Allies' front. With only a limited number of infantry and armored vehicles to challenge the well-prepared Allied troops, the attack failed but, in the days to come, as the German panzer divisions raced toward the area north and east of Caen, the fighting became much harder and more costly for both sides.

Standartenführer Kurt Meyer.

EYEWITNESS

I spent the first night on the beach with my truck. You know what that means? There were dead bodies to be moved, so that they didn't affect the morale of the troops landing the next day.
Sapper G. Wilson, 72nd Field Company, Royal Engineers

The 716th Coastal Defense Division, under the command of General Richter, had been decimated by the Allied invasion on D-Day. This allowed the Canadians to reinforce their positions and continue their advance on June 7th, without too much enemy interference. The front line ran from Norray-en-Bessin, across the main Caen-Bayeux railway track and highway, to Bretteville-l'Orgueilleuse and back to Le Fresne-Camilly. Further east, part of the 9th Brigade advanced toward Carpiquet, taking Les Buissons and Buron by noon. But as they advanced toward Franqueville, the 12th SS Panzer Division launched a counterattack.

Led by Standartenführer Kurt "Panzermeyer" Meyer, commander of the 25th SS Panzer Grenadier Regiment, two battalions, with tanks in support, were launched against the Canadians on June 7th. Meyer had watched the Canadians approach from his observation post in the Abbaye

German anti-aircraft defenses in the area around Caen.

Ardenne and knew just where to strike for maximum effect. The Canadians were forced back and the Germans recaptured Buron. Just as they did so, however, *HMS Belfast* laid down a barrage and the Canadians immediately countered the German attack. After the panzer attack was successfully broken up, Buron was once again taken by the Canadians – but it had cost them over 400 casualties and twenty-one tanks. The

Canadians' swift advance from the beaches had finally been checked. And to the east, just north of Caen, the British advance from Sword Beach was also grinding to a halt.

During the German offensive, a company from the 12th SS Panzer Division managed to cross the railroad and take part of Putot-en-Bessin. Following a rolling artillery barrage, the Canadians were able to push the Germans back with an armored counterattack, but in their retreat the Germans took with them sixty-four prisoners from the Royal Winnipeg Rifles. The Canadian prisoners were taken, under guard, into the grounds of the Château d'Audrieu. The wounded were placed in the center of the group and all were made to wait. At some point in the next few hours an SS staff officer ordered a halftrack and machine gun to the scene. The prisoners, including the wounded, were then slaughtered in cold blood. It was the start of a series of incidents by the fanatical SS troops; later the same day, forty-eight Canadians from the Queen's Own Rifles were also murdered by the SS in the grounds of Meyer's HQ at the Abbaye Ardenne.

Over the next few days, the battle raged over the same ground with few gains on either side. A week after D-Day the British, Canadian, and German troops were dug-in and waiting for sufficient supplies and reinforcements to launch a major attack. As the Americans raced for Cherbourg, Montgomery had to decide how best to re-launch his attack on Caen. His Anglo-Canadian troops now faced some of Germany's best trained and battle-hardened troops who were quite determined in the execution of their tasks. Montgomery's troops also faced the superior armor of the panzer divisions, led by strong and resolute commanders who had learned the lessons of war the hard way during their fight against the Russians on the Eastern Front.

Operation Perch (see Chapter 6) had shown how difficult it was to break out from the Bocage, and with Monty trying to build up his supplies (which had suffered a serious set-back during the storms of June 19th to 21st), the next major offensive wasn't launched until Operation Epsom on June 26th (see Chapter 5). When Operation Epsom failed, General Crocker, commander of British I Corps, ordered the Canadians to launch Operation Windsor on July 4th. The objective of Operation Windsor was to take the airfield and village at Carpiquet. Over 400 guns laid down a artillery barrage prior to the attack and, in addition, the 16-inch guns of *HMS Rodney* and 15-inch guns of *HMS Roberts* along with two squadrons of rocket firing Typhoons were used to soften up the German defenses. The village was taken but the defenses around the hangers on the airfield proved too strong to penetrate. Despite several German counterattacks to retake the village, the Canadians managed to hold their positions until July 8th when Operation Charnwood, the main offensive against Caen, was launched.

EYEWITNESS

We fired at the village with 50 kilogram mortar bombs which were part explosive and part incendiary. They had been part of the airfield defense long before the landings, and when our Werfer Regiment got them ready for action, they obviously caused considerable casualties. The enemy kept very quiet here for the next few days; even during the great attack on Caen, they stayed on the defenses. However our own attempt to retake Carpiquet from Franqueville failed.

Obersturmbannführer H. Meyer, staff officer, 12th SS Panzer Grenadier Regiment

Caen in 1944 and 1999. Probably the same street.

After the vicious fighting the Canadians had endured, Montgomery decided to carpet bomb Caen to disrupt the German defenses before he sent in the ground troops. On the night of July 7th nearly 500 Lancaster and Halifax bombers dropped over 2,500 tons of bombs onto northern Caen. The following morning Operation Charnwood was launched: the British 3rd Infantry Division on the left, the British 59th Division in the center, and the Canadian 3rd Infantry Division on the right attacked along an eight-mile front.

Bomber Command insisted that a 5,500-meter safety margin should be kept between the front line Allied troops and the bombing zone. Subsequently, the villages to the north of Caen, which the Germans had spent the past month fortifying, remained untouched by the bombardment. Though the German support units undoubtedly suffered greatly in the bombings, this fact had little affect on the forward troops other than the psychological effect of seeing the Allies' undoubted air superiority.

After a full day's fighting the British managed to break their way through the villages and enter the city by the evening. The previous night's bombing proved to be counter-productive: the streets were so full of rubble and stone that it was impossible for the armor to advance until the area was cleared. This gave the Germans the opportunity to make the best of their retreat. The Canadians, attacking along the Caen–Bayeux highway, reached the River Orne only to find all the bridges blown and the Germans well-entrenched in the rubble of the southern suburbs. Caen may have fallen, but the Germans still blocked Montgomery's breakout.

By mid-July the Allies were stretched to their limits. The Americans were becoming bogged down and the British and Canadians appeared to be at a stalemate around Caen. With no guarantee of winning a war of attrition and the need to keep the German Panzer divisions in the west,★ Montgomery decided to make a bold thrust through the British Airborne sector in order to re-establish the threat of a breakout and keep the Germans on the defensive. Thus Operation Goodwood was born, and, under the diversion of this operation, the Americans would launch Operation Cobra – an attempt at breakout in the west.

The Canadian part in Operation Goodwood was codenamed

★*Intelligence at that time suggested that the German infantry divisions arriving in Normandy were being deployed against the British and Canadian sector so that the armored Panzer Divisions could be relocated and used against the Americans.*

Operation Atlantic. While the British launched their three armored brigades toward Bourguébus and Falaise, the British 51st and Canadian 3rd Infantry Divisions would protect their left flank. Canadian II Corps, under the command of Lieutenant General G. Simonds would, at the same time, protect their right flank by clearing the southern suburbs of Caen.

EYEWITNESS

Then began the most terrifying hours of our lives . . . . Among the thunder of the explosions, we could hear the wounded screams and the insane howling of men who had been driven mad . . . . The stunning effect temporarily incapacitated everyone. Nerves, emotions were drained; it was a wild moon landscape of brown craters, wreathed in the acrid smell of high-explosives. Tanks caught fire; tanks were buried; men were buried; a 60 ton Tiger was blown upside down. And still the RAF poured overhead, the great black painted night bombers roaring low to make certain of their aim.

W. Kortenhaus, wireless operator, 21st Panzer Division

At 0500 on July 18th, 1000 Lancasters carpet-bombed the ground on either side of the armored thrust with payloads of 500 and 1000 pound bombs. Fragmentation bombs were used in an attempt to reduce the amount of cratering and inflict maximum casualties to the troops on the ground.

Despite the mass bombing, the armored thrust of Operation Goodwood soon ground to a halt when it came up against the Germans' well-positioned artillery. The Canadians, however, had more success and managed to reach their objectives. By the end of the day, they had crossed the River Orne and cleared the southern and eastern parts of Caen including the villages of Colembelles and Mondeville, The following day the villages of Louvigny and Fleury-sur-Orne also fell to the Canadians.

By July 20th, the Allies had managed to form a solid front line that now encircled Caen. The Canadians were given one final task as part of Operation Atlantic – to take the ridge at Verrières. A delay in moving the British 7th Armored Brigade out and moving the Canadian troops in, gave the Germans time to reinforce their position and the attack failed at a cost of over 500 men.

On the same day, Nazi Germany found itself in a state of turmoil and confusion. Oberst Count Klaus von Stauffenberg, an influential officer of the Wehrmacht, had chosen this day to plant a bomb in a conference room at Hitler's HQ as part of a well-detailed plot to assassinate the dictator and take power away from the Nazis. It was hoped that, with the evil dictator gone, a moderate government could negotiate a peace deal with the Allies and save Germany from complete and utter destruction.

Hitler, however, survived the blast and quickly launched an inquiry into the conspiracy. The consequences of this inquiry had repercussions that would be felt all over the Nazi-dominated continent. After the execution and disgrace of those who had dared to conspire against the Führer, surviving military personnel decided it would be wiser to follow orders, for fear of being linked with the "Plot of July 20th." The resolution of Germany's troops was now set in stone. It would be total victory or total defeat with no room for compromise. The war would now be fought to the bitter end.

With the Americans about to launch their breakthrough in the west, Montgomery was not prepared to let the British and Canadian troops become bogged down in another stalemate. The attempt to break out would continue and the next phase of operations was passed onto Lieutenant General Crerar, commander of the Canadian First Army. To begin, the Canadian Corps would launch Operation Spring on July 24th in an attempt to take the objectives originally scheduled for Operation Goodwood. This would

From the right: Feldmarschall von Rundstedt; Sturmbannführer Hubert Meyer; Obergruppenführer Sepp Dietrich; Oberführer Fritz Witt; Standartenführer Kurt Meyer.

then be followed by an attack down the Caen-Falaise road. Operation Spring was a night offensive, so to aid visibility for the Allied troops, hundreds of searchlights were focused on low-lying clouds, a revolutionary illumination technique known as "Monty's Moonlight." The overall effect was to create an artificial moonlight over the battlefield.

The Canadians pushed southward toward May-sur-Orne, Verrières, and Tilly-la-Campagne and the battle raged for several days. Though Operation Spring was meant to be the start of the British-Canadian breakout toward Falaise, at the same time the attack kept the German armor engaged while the Americans made their breakout in the west. Montgomery also moved the British Second Army further west and launched Operation Bluecoat (see Chapter 6) in an attempt to further protect the American advance.

The Allies realized in early August that the disposition of the German forces at that time presented an opportunity to push forward, and possibly, with a series of well-planned and timed offensives, encircle the enemy. With such a plan in mind, Patton's Third Army was ordered to push northward toward Argentan, rather than eastward, while the Canadians pushed south toward Falaise.

The lessons learned in previous operations were taken into account when the II Canadian Corps Commander, Lieutenant General Simonds, planned the next offensive, Operation Totalize. On the night of August 7th, Bomber Command laid down a massive aerial bombardment of over 3,000 tons of bombs, prior to an armored attack. As the troops and tanks moved toward their objective, they were guided by the tracer fire from Bofors 40mm anti-aircraft guns into a battlefield illuminated by Monty's moonlight. Within the first hour of the advance 60,000 artillery shells had been fired into the German positions.

The attack advanced down either side of the Caen-Falaise road (N-158). To the west a Canadian armored brigade, infantry brigade, and reconnaissance regiment pushed through the village of Rocquancourt and captured the high ground at Bretteville-sur-Orne. In the meantime, another brigade followed up on foot and cleared the villages of May-sur-Orne, Fontenay, and Rocquancourt. To the east, brigades of the 51st Highland Division mopped up the villages of Tilly-la-Campagne, La Hogue, and Sequeville. With these objectives secured, the Germans' main defensive line was broken and the first phase of the operation was complete. This was achieved by noon on the 8th, a feat no doubt helped by the transfer of a great deal of German armor from the Anglo-Canadian front in order to counterattack the Americans at Mortain.

At one point during the night, Meyer, the commander of the 12th SS Panzer Division, had personally challenged some of the German infantrymen who had begun retreating from their positions around Cintheaux. The foot soldiers were forced back to their positions and Meyer reinforced them with armor and anti-tank guns. In the afternoon of August 8th the second phase of Operation Totalize commenced.

A German SS trooper with a lethal MG 42.

The US 8th Air Force dropped 1,500 tons of bombs on the German defenses. Some of the supplies were dropped short of their target and caused over 300 hundred casualties among the 1st Polish Armored Division and 3rd Canadian Division. Despite this, the attack continued.

By August 12th, Generalfeldmarschall von Kluge, commander in chief, in the West, decided to withdraw his troops from Mortain. To the north and east the Allied advance had ground to a halt as the Canadian and British troops became exhausted and battle-weary. The front line had been extended to Vimont in the east, to Quesnay on the Caen-Falaise road in the west, and the British and Canadian

A German magazine cover promises that "German counter-measures are being prepared" for the Invasion.

troops had linked up. As the men rested General Simonds had already prepared his plans for a follow-up operation codenamed Tractable.

To the south, the Americans had reached the town of Argentan on August 13th and were preparing to advance toward Falaise. At that moment an order came down from General Bradley that the Americans must halt and not cross the boundary between the 12th and 21st Army Groups for fear that the two armies might, accidentally, end up fighting each other. Thus the American advance northward was stopped.

With the British Second Army fighting their way through some of the most difficult terrain in Normandy, progress had been very slow. The task of sealing off the Falaise Gap was left to the troops of 1st Canadian Army.

On August 14th, Operation Tractable was launched but initially made slow progress. Once again, during the aerial bombardment that preceded the assault, the infantry suffered over 300 casualties as a result of the bombs falling onto Allied positions. The bombings also destroyed some of the bridges over the River Laison and so, by the evening, the Canadians were still three miles short of Falaise.

The next day the Canadians crossed the River Dives at Jort and headed south toward Trun. They also crossed the Falaise to St Pierre-sur-Dives road (D-511).

On August 16th, there were only twenty-four kilometers between the Canadian and American armies. In an area some fifty-six kilometers deep, the remnants of the German 7th Army and 5th Panzer Army were being squeezed into an ever-decreasing pocket. Some 100,000 German soldiers were now retreating toward the Seine under the protection of the SS Panzer units who provided a rearguard. Montgomery issued an order for the Americans to advance toward Chambois, and the neck of the pocket was reduced to no more than eleven kilometers when the Canadians entered the bombed out ruins of Falaise, where small groups of the 12th SS Panzer were holding out.

In the meantime Generalfeldmarschall von Kluge was missing and Hitler had appointed Generalfeldmarschall Model, "Savior of the Eastern Front," as his successor. On his return to duty von Kluge was issued orders to return to Germany and, a few days later, on his journey back, he committed suicide.

The Germans counterattacked the US 90th Division at Le-Bourg-St-Léonard, on August 16th, forcing them out of the village. The following day the Americans countered with probing attacks in the direction of Chambois and decided to launch a main assault the next day. During this time the Canadian and Polish divisions pushed on toward Trun, St Lambert-sur-Dives, and Chambois, while the British closed in from the west.

Two days later, the RAF flew over 1,400 sorties against the retreating Germans. Rocket-firing Typhoons flew in and knocked out the leading and rear vehicles of a column and then returned to destroy the vehicles trapped in between. After the Typhoons had done their work, Spitfires would strafe the area with cannon and machine gun fire.

German prisoners from the 12th SS (Hitler Jugend) Division.

By the end of the day the Falaise pocket was reduced to less than eleven kilometers deep and twelve kilometers wide; over 1,000 vehicles and nearly 100 tanks had been destroyed within the area.

Earlier that day Major DV Currie was given the order to take the village of St Lambert-sur-Dives with a company from the Sutherland Highlanders of Canada and a squadron of tanks from the 19th Canadian Recce Regiment. Their attack started in the evening of Friday, August 18th at 1800. The following day, while Major Currie's men battled on in the village, an historic event occurred. In the early evening, about three kilometers down the road at Chambois, men of the Polish 10th Mounted Rifle Regiment and the American 359th Infantry Division made the first link-up across the Falaise Gap. The Canadians arrived on the scene a short time later.

Inside the pocket the blood-letting continued. Argentan had fallen to the Americans, but, despite the link-up at Chambois the Germans still had an escape route about three kilometers wide between St. Lambert-sur-Dives and Chambois. This escape route, however, was blocked by the River Dives. The river was not wide, but its banks were too steep to allow vehicles to cross. Only three crossing points existed — two small bridges west of St Lambert-sur-Dives and a ford at Moissy. Since all the roads leading to the bridge passed through the village of Tournai-sur-Dives, the retreating German forces were forced into a bottleneck that was only a few hundred meters wide. This was known to the Allies and they concentrated their firepower into the killing zone. The area soon became known to the Germans as "Das Korridor des Todes" [The Corridor of Death].

EYEWITNESS

The sweat ran into my smarting eyes and my old head wound opened. There was a continual bombardment registering bull's-eyes every time. The Canadian and Polish guns found our range and could not miss. The whole country was saturated with dead or wounded German soldiers.
Standartenführer Kurt Meyer, commander, 12th SS Panzer Division

Germans that survived the corridor had to fight their way past Mont Ormel — an 800-foot-high mace-shaped ridge, which the Poles had taken — in order to reach the 2nd SS Panzer Corps who now held the German front line. The Poles had a commanding view of the retreating German army and fired onto the streams of German soldiers, tanks, and vehicles that passed either side of the ridge they held. But by August 20th, the Poles had become isolated and they were under constant counterattack by SS troops desperate to protect the remnants of their battered army. The fighting continued all day, but the Poles held their ground and finally repulsed the last German counterattack in the evening. Around them, the cost of the battle was all too evident, as 300 of their Polish comrades lay dead or wounded.

Nevertheless, the Germans would not abandon their efforts. The next morning they launched another series of attacks up the southwestern slopes of the ridge. As the Falaise Gap continued to close around them, the German attacks became more desperate; their bold infantry attacks, however, proved fruitless and German soldiers were massacred by the overwhelming Polish defenses.

A few hours later the Canadians established firm contact with the Poles on the ridge and, to the west, the Americans joined forces with the British at Villedieu-lès-Bailleul. At Trun, the British and Canadians were also consolidated. And, in St Lambert-sur-Dives, Major Currie's men had finally beaten the fanatical SS troops who had fought to keep the corridor open for their comrades. With his force of only fifteen tanks and fifty-five infantrymen Major Currie had been able to outmaneuver and overpower the mighty German Tiger tanks that defended the village. For this action Currie was later awarded the Victoria Cross. By August 21st the Falaise Gap had been well and truly sealed.

EYEWITNESS

When we came to St Lambert it was a neat small quiet French village, and when we left, it was a fantastic mess. The clutter of equipment, dead horses, wounded, dying and dead Germans, had turned it into a hell hole. It seems incredible that such devastation could be wrought in such a short space of time.

Major D. V. Currie, 29th (Canadian) Armored Reconnaissance Regiment

Though no accurate figures were ever recorded of how many Germans passed through the Gap and escaped to fight again, most military historians put the figure at around 50,000 soldiers. Similarly, it is estimated that another 50,000 were taken prisoner and that more than 10,000 German corpses littered the battlefield. Operational research teams assessed the number of enemy transport and weapons destroyed or abandoned in the area. The totals were: in the American sector – 220 tanks, 160 SP guns, 700+ pieces of artillery, and 5,000 vehicles; in the British, Canadian, and Polish sector – 187 armored fighting vehicles and SP guns, 157 armored cars or personnel carriers, 1,778 lorries, 669 cars, and 252 pieces of ordnance. A few days after the fighting had stopped General Eisenhower went to see the carnage for himself.

EYEWITNESS

I was conducted through it on foot, to encounter scenes that could be described only by Dante. It was literally possible to walk for hundreds of yards at a time, stepping on nothing but dead and decaying flesh.
General Dwight Eisenhower, supreme commander of the Allied Expeditionary Force

Of the fifty divisions Hitler had committed to the fighting in Normandy since June 6th, 1944, only ten could now still be considered fighting units. The German army had been almost decimated. On August 22nd, 1944 the battle for Normandy was finally over.

CIRCUIT SEVEN

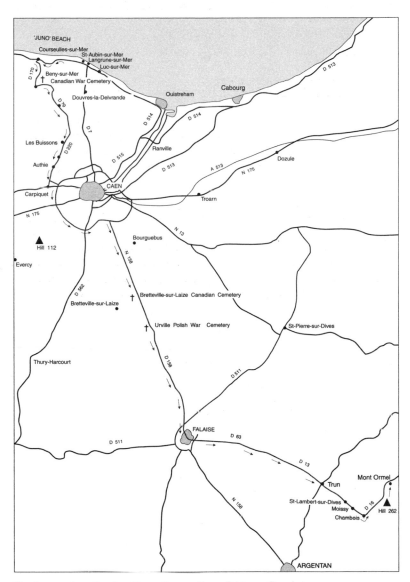

Circuit seven. Juno Beach – Courseilles-sur-Mer – Falaise – Chambois

JUNO BEACH STARTS AT LANGRUNE-SUR-MER in the east and runs through to Ver-sur-Mer in the west. Driving east to west the sections are codenamed: Nan, Mike, and Love. This section of beach is along the D-514. As you pass through Langrune-sur-Mer, a memorial stone on your right is dedicated to No. 48 (RM) Commando who attacked a German strongpoint here on June 6th, 1944. Continue through Langrune-sur-Mer, into St Aubin-sur-Mer, and along the narrow high street. On the right, as the beach area comes into view, you will see a 50mm gun still in its concrete emplacement. Note how the seaward-facing side of the bunker is protected by a solid reinforced concrete wall, while the slit has been constructed so that the gun can still direct its fire along the beach. On the right side is a memorial to the Canadian North Shore Regiment and, nearby, there is a memorial to the Fort Garry Horse (10th Armored Regiment) and to No. 48 (RM) Commando.

Continue along the D-514, through Bernières-sur-Mer (look out for the large half-timbered house, on your right, which has been featured many times in original photographs of the D-Day Juno Beach landings), to Courseulles-sur-Mer. Take the first right and then the fourth left turn and drive to the end of the road. As you approach the harbor, there is a Sherman tank on your left. Park nearby and return to look at the plaques on the side of the tank. This is a DD tank (one of the AVREs explained in Chapter 5) which had belonged to the 1st Hussars. It was salvaged from the sea, restored, and dedicated in 1971. Across the road there is a German 50mm gun standing by the edge of the harbor. It was on this side of the harbor (which is also the mouth of the River Seulles) that The Regina Rifles and 6th (Canadian) Armored Regiment (1st Hussars) landed on the morning of June 6th.

Drive over the swing bridge across the harbor (if the barrier is down at the bridge you can take the road to the left and drive around the harbor) and rejoin the D-514. Continue along the road and cross the bridge over the River Seulles. Turn right at the next crossroads and drive down to the beach. The beach from here back to Courseulles-sur-Mer was codenamed "Mike Red" and this is where The Royal Winnipeg Rifles, the 6th (Canadian) Armored Regiment, and two troops of the 26th Assault Squadron, Royal Engineers, came ashore on D-Day.

Near the beach you will see another AVRE, a Petard tank that belonged to the 79th Armored Division. This particular Petard has a remarkable and well-documented history. Some of the Petard tanks, including this one, also used to carry a fascine, (a large bundle of wood used to fill in ditches or craters). After it landed on the beach this tank made its way to a flooded culvert in order to drop in its fascine, but then the tank slid and nose-dived into the culvert. Within seconds the tank sank beneath the water, but the crew managed to get out safely and find cover in the sand dunes.

The fascine was released from the tank by the troop commander and an ARC (Armored Ramp Carrier) was brought up and laid its bridging equipment on top of the tank. In the meantime, a mortar bomb fell in among the tank crew sheltering in the sand dunes, killing two of them and badly wounding the driver, William Dunn. The tank remained buried in the sand for over thirty years until 1976 when it was taken out and restored to its former glory. That same year William Dunn and another surviving veteran, Bill Hawkins, returned to Juno Beach to witness the dedication of the tank as a memorial to the D-Day landings.

Further along the beach is one of the monuments of the Comité du Débarquement and to the right, on top of the sand dune, a giant cross of Lorraine. It was at this beach exit that General Montgomery came ashore. Winston Churchill also landed here on June 12th followed by Charles de Gaulle on June 14th, and His Majesty King George VI two days later.

Return to Courseulles-sur-Mer and drive into the center. Take the D-170 for Reviers and at the crossroads, in the center of the village, turn left onto the D-35. One kilometer on the left is the Beny-sur-Mer Canadian War Cemetery, Reviers. Buried here are some 2,043 Canadians, mainly from the 3rd Canadian Infantry Division, 3 British soldiers, an airman, and 1 French soldier. 335 men of the 3rd Canadian Infantry Division were killed on D-Day and many more were lost as they fought their way toward Carpiquet and Caen. This cemetery has two observation towers, which give a stunning bird's-eye view of the cemetery and, on a clear day, the sea just off Juno Beach.

From the cemetery continue to drive along the D-35 and turn right onto the D-79 toward Beny-sur-Mer. This village was captured in the afternoon of D-Day and there is a memorial to Lé Régiment de la Chaudière in the village. Continue along the D-79 through Basly, where there is another memorial to the Canadians. Past Colomby-sur-Thaon, turn right onto the D-220 and drive through the village of Villons-les-Buissons. At the next junction, leading to Les Buissons, is a monument to the 9th Brigade, 3rd Canadian Infantry Division. This place was named "Hell's Corner" and it was from here that the 9th Brigade launched their attack toward Carpiquet on June 7th. As they passed through Buron and Authie, Standartenführer Kurt Meyer launched his counterattack and stopped the Canadian advance.

Continue to drive along the D-220, the same route taken by the 9th Armored Brigade, onto the D-14 (passing under the N-13) and into Carpiquet. In each of the villages – Buron, Authie, and Carpiquet – you will find memorials to the Canadians.

Warning!
Though the design of the two observation towers is aesthetically pleasing, the steps leading up to them are not very practical and great care should taken when climbing and descending.

Drive back along the D-14 and take the N-13 toward Caen. Turn right onto the Caen périphérique (counter-clockwise) and take the third exit toward Falaise on the D-158. About twelve kilometers south of Caen on the right hand side of the road is the Bretteville-sur-Laize Canadian War Cemetery. Follow the signs from the D-158 to the cemetery.

This second Canadian War Cemetery has 2,958 graves, of which 2,872 are Canadian, 80 British, 4 Australian, 1 New Zealander and 1 French. Those who are buried here were killed as they fought to close the Falaise Gap. There is someone from nearly every unit of Canadian II Corps buried in the cemetery.

Four kilometers further along the D-158, again on the right, is Urville Polish War Cemetery. This cemetery has 696 graves and is the only Polish National Cemetery in France.

Return to the D-158 and drive into Falaise. In Falaise visit the "Musée d'Aout 1944 de la Bataille de la Poche de Falaise." This museum retraces the route taken by the Allied armies during August 1944 and explains how the Falaise Gap was sealed. There is also a selection of uniforms, weapons, vehicles, and photographs on display.

From Falaise take the D-63, which runs into the D-13 to Trun, and continute to the village of St Lambert-sur-Dives. On the right hand side as you enter the village a marker commemorates Major D. Currie who was awarded the Victoria Cross for his action in St Lambert -sur-Dives. Continue through the village to Chambois. As you pass through the small hamlet of Moissy (not marked on most maps) the road to the right leads to the ford over the River Dives. The road to the left was used by the Germans to bypass the Polish strongpoint at Mont Ormel. This is the route that the Germans called "The Corridor of Death."

Finally, to end the tour, drive into Chambois and turn left onto the D-16. At the crossroads, a memorial marker explains the closing of the Falaise Gap. Continue along the D-16 to Mont Ormel and visit the Polish Memorial that stands on Hill 262. The hill offers a magnificent view of the Dives Valley and the corridor through which the Germans tried to escape.

MILITARY ABBREVIATIONS AND SLANG

ARC	Armored Ramp Carrier. Specially adapted tank for laying ramps across ditches, tanks, etc.
AVRE	Armored Vehicle, Royal Engineers
BAR	Browning Automatic Rifle. An American light machine gun.
COSSAC	Chief of Staff to the Supreme Allied Commander
CSM	Company Sergeant Major
DD	Duplex drive. DUKWS (see next) were fitted with duplex drive, which made it possible for them to move by land or sea.
DUKW	Amphibious Landing Craft
DZ	Drop Zone
FLAK	Fleiger Abwehrkanone. German acronym for anti-aircraft guns.
GI	Strictly speaking, Government Issue. In common usage, GI refers to individual American soldiers.
GOC	General Officer Commanding
HQ	Headquarters
IR	Infantry Regiment (see also PIR)
LCA	Landing Craft Assault
LCOCU	Landing Craft Obstacle Clearance Units. The units charged with clearing a safe path through the mines and other obstructions that guarded the beaches.
LCT	Landing Craft Tanks
LCT(R)	Landing Craft Tanks (Rockets)
LCVP	Landing Craft Vehicles and Personnel

Para/para	Parachute/parachute
PB	Parachute Battalion
PIAT	Projector, Infantry, Anti-Tank. Similar to a bazooka.
PIR	Parachute Infantry Regiment
PLUTO	Pipe Line under the Ocean. Flexible pipelines laid under the ocean by the Allies to pump petrol, oil, and water directly to the Continental battlefields.
RAF	Royal Air Force
RE	Royal Engineers
Recce	Reconnaissance
RM	Royal Marines
SHAEF	Supreme Headquarters of the Allied Expeditionary Force
SP	Self-Propelled (as in SP guns, for example)
VC	Victoria Cross. The highest British military award for bravery.

Select Bibliography

For those who would like to know more about the background to the battles of D-Day and the Normandy campaign, we can recommend the following:

Ambrose, Stephen. *The Supreme Commander: The War Years of General Dwight D. Eisenhower.* (New York, 1970)

Arnold, General HH. *Global Mission.* (London, 1951).

Austin, AB. *Landed at Dawn.* (London, 1943)

Balfour, Michael. *Propaganda in War, 1939-45.* (London, 1979)

Blumenson, Martin. *Eisenhower.* (New York, 1972)

Blumenstritt, General Gunther. *Rundstedt, the Soldier and the Man.* (London, 1952)

Bryant, Sir Arthur. *Triumph in the West, 1943-45.* (London, 1959)

Burgett, Donald. *As Eagles Screamed.* (New York, 1979)

Burns, James. *Roosevelt: The Soldier of Freedom.* (London, 1971); *By Air to Battle: The Official Account of the British First and Sixth Airborne Divisions.* (London, HMSO, 1945); *Canada's Battle in Normandy.* (Ottawa, King's Printer, 1946)

Chalfont, Alun. *Montgomery of Alamein.* (London, 1976)

Chatterton, Brigadier George. *The Wings of Pegasus.* (London, 1962).

Churchill, Sir Winston. *The Second World War* (6 vols). (London, 1948-54)

Clay, Major Ewart. *The Path of the 50th.* (Aldershot, 1950)

Dank, Milton. *The Glider Gang.* (London, 1978)

Durnford-Slater, John. *Commando.* (London, 1953)

Eisenhower, General Dwight. *Crusade in Europe.* (London, 1949); *Fourth Infantry Division.* (Baton Rouge,1946)

Freidin, Seymour and Richardson William, (eds.). *The Fatal Decisions. (New York, 1956).*

Gale, Lieutenant General Richard. *With the Sixth Airborne Division in Normandy.* (London, 1948)

Golley; John. *The Big Drop: The Guns of Merville.* (New York, 1982)

Harrison, Michael. *Mulberry: The Return in Triumph.* (London, 1965)

Hastings, Max. *Overlord.* (London, 1984).

Howard, Michael. *British Intelligence in the Second World War* (6 vols). London, HMSO, 1990.

Irving, David. *The Rise and Fall of the Luftwaffe.* (London, 1974)

Keegan, John. *Six Armies in Normandy.* (London, 1982)

Ladd, James. *Commandos and Rangers of World War II.* (New York, 1978)

Mackesy, Kenneth. *Armoured Crusader: General Sir Percy Hobart.* (London, 1967)

Majdalany, Fred. *The Fall of Fortress Europe.* (London, 1969)

Messenger, Charles. *The Commandos, 1940-1946.* (London, 1985)

Michie, Allan. *The Invasion of Europe.* (London, 1965)

Mollo, Andrew. *The Armed Forces of World War II.* (London, 1981)

Morgan, Lieutenant General Sir Frederick. *Overture to Overlord.* (London, 1950)

Morris, James. *History of the US Army.* (London 1986)

Norman, Albert. *Operation Overlord.* (Harrisburg, 1952)

North, John. *North-West Europe.* (London, 1953)

Norton, GG. *The Red Devils.* (London, 1971)

Otway, Colonel Terence. *The Second World War, 1939-45: Airborne Forces.* (London, 1946)

Peis, Gunther. *The Mirror of Deception*. (London, 1977)

Perrault, Gilles. *The Secrets of D-Day*. (London, 1965)

Pitt, Barrie and Frances. *The Month-by-Month Atlas of World War II*. (New York, 1989)

Pogue, Forrest. *The Supreme Command*. (Washington, DC, 1946)

Ruppenthal, Major Roland. *Utah to Cherbourg* (Washington, DC, 1946)

Saunders, Hilary St George. *The Green Beret*. (London, 1949)
The Red Beret. (London, 1950)

Scarfe, Norman. *Assault Division*. (London, 1947)

Shapiro, Lionel. *The Sixth of June*. (London, 1956)

Stacey, Colonel CP. *The Canadian Army, 1939-45* (5 vols). (Ottawa, King's Printers, 1960)

Turner, John. *Invasion 1944*. (London, 1959).

Warner, Philip. *The D-Day Landings*. (London, 1980)

Weller, George. *The Story of the Paratroops*. (New York, 1958)

Wertenbaker, Charles. *Invasion!* (New York, 1944)

Willmott, HP. *June 1944*. (Dorset, England, 1984)

Woollcombe, Robert. *Lion Rampant*. (London, 1970)

THE ORDER OF BATTLE

The unit organization chart that follows is necessarily somewhat arbitrary. The size and composition of units in the field varied and was constantly changing according to their structure (there are more men in an infantry unit than an armored unit, e.g.), their immediate task, (special task units may be added or removed), or their casualties in battle.

The basic fighting unit of both the Allied and German armies in northwest Europe was the division, but the exact make up of a division was subject to constant tinkering by both sides. The numbers given below are good working averages and should be treated. By 1944/45, the Brigade was no longer part of the general organizational but was still used for special units usually assigned specific tasks.

Unit Type:	Usually comprised of:	Usually commanded by:	Approximate number of men:
Army Group	2-3 Armies	General	300,000
Army	2-4 Corps	Lieutenant General	100,000
Corps	2-5 Divisions	Major General	30,000
Division	2-3 Brigades	Major General	15,500
Brigade	3 Regiments	Brigadier General	7,500

Unit Type:	Usually comprised of:	Usually commanded by:	Approximate number of men:
Regiment	3 Battalions	Colonel or Brigadier General	2,500
Battalion	3 Companies	Lieutenant Colonel	800
Company	3 platoons	Captain	180
Platoon	3 Squads	Lieutenant	40-50
Squad	2 sections	Sergeant	
Section		Corporal	

Interlink's Bestselling
Travel Publications

THE TRAVELLER'S HISTORY SERIES

"An excellent series of brief histories."

—*The New York Times*

The Traveller's History series is designed for travellers who want more historical background on the country they are visiting than can be found in a tour guide. Each volume offers a complete and authoritative history of the country from the earliest times up to the present day. A Gazetteer cross-referenced to the main text pinpoints the historical importance of sights and towns. Illustrated with maps and line drawings, this literate and lively series makes ideal before-you-go reading, and is just as handy tucked into suitcase or backpack.

A Traveller's History of Australia	$14.95 pb
A Traveller's History of the Caribbean	$14.95 pb
A Traveller's History of China	$14.95 pb
A Traveller's History of England	$14.95 pb
A Traveller's History of France	$14.95 pb
A Traveller's History of Greece	$14.95 pb
A Traveller's History of India	$14.95 pb
A Traveller's History of Ireland	$14.95 pb
A Traveller's History of Italy	$14.95 pb
A Traveller's History of Japan	$14.95 pb
A Traveller's History of London	$14.95 pb
A Traveller's History of North Africa	$15.95 pb
A Traveller's History of Paris	$14.95 pb
A Traveller's History of Russia	$14.95 pb
A Traveller's History of Scotland	$14.95 pb
A Traveller's History of Spain	$14.95 pb
A Traveller's History of Turkey	$14.95 pb
A Traveller's History of the U.S.A.	$14.95 pb